MW00667987

PROBLEMS IN CIVILIZATION

David H. Pinkney

General Editor

PROBLEMS IN CIVILIZATION

EUROPEAN EMPIRE BUILDING

Nineteenth-Century Imperialism

Edited with
an Introduction by

William B. Cohen

Indiana University

FORUM PRESS

Copyright © 1980 by Forum Press, St. Louis, Missouri. All rights reserved.
No part of this work may be reproduced or transmitted in any form or by
any means, electronic or mechanical, including photocopying and record-
ing, or by any information storage or retrieval system, without permission
in writing from the publisher.

Published simultaneously in Canada.

Printed in the United States of America.

Library of Congress Catalog Card Number: 79-57459

ISBN: 0-88273-410-5

Arrival of French forces at Fashoda, 1898. A colonialist view.

—From P. Legendre, *Nos gloires coloniales* (Paris, 1906), p. 304.

CONTENTS

INTRODUCTION

OUR WORLD has been deeply affected by imperialism, particularly the European expansion of the late nineteenth century, which brought most of Asia and Africa under the white man's rule. Partly as a result of European military supremacy, Western values and institutions were imposed on these societies. In the end the colonies won their independence, but they did so largely by using notions of nationalism and self-determination against the colonizing powers. Even in eclipse, Europe has continued to shape the destiny of former dependencies, through the institutions and values left behind after colonization ended.

From the sixteenth century on, European power expanded to the four corners of the world. This advance was thought to have ended in the eighteenth century and even to have receded as the North American colonies achieved their independence, followed by the Latin American struggle for freedom in the early nineteenth century. Yet European expansion overseas actually continued: the British government gained control over India in 1857; France established itself in Algeria in 1830 and in Cochinchina in 1859. The tempo of expansion speeded up in the decades after 1880. This dramatic expansion is unrivaled in the history of European imperialism. Never before had so much territory been acquired simultaneously in such a brief period by so many European powers. Within a single generation Britain acquired an additional 4.7 million square miles of empire, with 88 million new subjects. Germany, in a short fifteen-year period, acquired an empire of 1 million square miles inhabited by 14 million people. Between 1880 and 1900 France added 3.5 million square miles and 37 million people to its empire. By 1900, half a billion people outside Europe, and half the non-European population of the world—one-third of humanity—lived under European rule. Historians have christened this unprecedented spurt of empire building the "new imperialism" to distinguish it from the overseas expansion of the maritime countries (Spain, Portugal, Holland, England, and France) in the sixteenth to eighteenth centuries. Late-nineteenth-century imperialism is commonly discussed in terms of the activities of the West European states. This book will adhere to that tradition. But the reader should be aware of the existence of other imperialisms at the same time. In the second half of the century Russia expanded east and south across its borders, and the United States, just as the century neared its end, annexed Hawaii, the Philippines, and Puerto Rico. African and Asian states became involved with their own imperialisms and carved impressive empires. Under pressure, however, these empires eventually disintegrated and fell to European rule.

European empire building occurred amid considerable controversy. Contemporaries argued over the wisdom of overseas expansion, claiming either that it was a costly waste of national resources or a safe investment for the future; that it brought bloodshed and mayhem overseas or that it was the means by which to "civilize" the "lower breeds of mankind"; that it weakened a nation's influence in the world by squandering resources, or that it was the underpinning of world power and influence. Historians have been equally divided on these questions, though some issues have lost their urgency in an age of decolonization, which has seen the destruction of the smug Eurocentric view of the world, so characteristic of the age of imperialism.

European statesmen acquired colonies piecemeal and thus took into consideration the economic virtues of individual pieces of real estate. But in asserting the need for acquiring a particular region, statesmen had very early made sweeping general claims about the advantages of overseas conquest. French Prime Minister Jules Ferry upheld the military expeditions to Tunisia in 1881 and to Tonkin and Madagascar in 1883-1885 in fairly similar terms. He cited the economic benefits that would accrue, the need to assert national prestige and glory, and the duty to spread civilization. Though the specifics varied according to time and place, expansionism was generally justified by familiar appeals to nationalism, profit, and power.

Contemporary critics and later historians have examined the self-serving claims of statesmen and wondered which claims accurately describe the true causes for expansion. Were the statements merely rhetorical appeals to the public of the day? The most influential interpretation of imperialism has been that of the English radical John Hobson, who wrote *Imperialism, A Study* (1902) in the midst of the Boer War, a conflict in which Britain tried to impose control over the European settlers of Dutch origin in South Africa. While he lists many influences, including nationalism and pressure by missionaries and other humanitarians, Hobson claims that the basic cause, "the taproot of imperialism," was economics. The rest were either ancillary causes or rationalizations. The respective needs of bankers and arms manufacturers for investments and markets made those groups impose a policy of overseas expansion on the home government. Hobson suggests that there were alternatives to imperialism. Excess capital could be used to pay workers more, thus leading to higher consumption and adequate profits for capitalists. Building on Hobson, the Russian revolutionary Vladimir Lenin went one step further. In *Imperialism, The Highest Stage of Capitalism* (1916), Lenin suggests that imperial expansion sprang from an internal necessity of capitalism. Without the new markets that empire provided, capitalism would already have collapsed, just as Karl Marx had predicted. This global explanation for empire has been attacked by a number of writers. Austrian economist Joseph Schumpeter suggested in 1919 that imperialism was not an expression of forces of capitalism but rather of "social atavisms," to the lingering feudal preference of military and bureaucratic elites for martial glory and territorial aggrandizement. He saw these values as contrary to capitalism's rationalism and spirit of calculation. If their ideas have not been accepted by all historians, Hobson, Lenin, and Schumpeter have nevertheless legitimated historians' search for monocausal explanations of the overseas expansion in the late nineteenth century. This approach essentially denies the multiplicity of factors.

Since the sixteenth century, European empire building had been part of a general expansion which included the growth of trade, wealth, and, after the mid-eighteenth century, population. European dynamism further increased in the nineteenth century in response to the industrial revolution. Europe was a society in full expansion, overflowing with products, capital, and population. Europe's population, which in 1815 had constituted 20 percent of the world total, by 1914 represented 27 percent. The growth of population led to massive emigration; between 1800 and 1930, Europe sent forty million permanent emigrants overseas. Most of these emigrants did not locate in the empires built at the end of the nineteenth century but settled instead in the United States, Canada, and Latin America.

Population was only one way in which Europe spread its influence. European traders, shippers, missionaries, and explorers were to be found in all corners of the earth. Massive capital flowed out of the banks of Berlin, Paris, and London, and most of it went to countries that offered a relatively safe return; comparatively little went to the new, as yet undeveloped colonies. All this activity indicates a dynamic, vibrant society that saw the entire globe as its field of action. Even if Europe did not intend to conquer the globe militarily, its expansion of population, trade, capital, and culture was gradually bringing the rest of the world into some form of dependency on it.

Europe's growing military power gave it the capacity to subjugate the peoples of Africa and Asia. Ever since the sixteenth century the armed ships of Western Europe had held mastery of the world's sea routes. At times they had imposed European control over coastal areas and had even launched successful inland conquests. The industrial

revolution created a still greater disproportion of wealth and power between the
European and non-European worlds. If, in
the earlier era, there had been a kind of
uneasy standoff between Europeans and the
peoples of Africa and Asia, the industrial
revolution sealed the latter's fate. There
could no longer be any doubt as to who
would be the victor. Small groups of Europeans, armed with industrially produced
firearms, had a potential military advantage
over Africans and Asians, who relied on
weapons made by artisans. In the seventeenth century European armies instituted
new methods of organization that relied on a
professional officer corps; soldiers were
trained to obey orders from their superiors.
This modern type of army could take on
forces many times larger which were organized in a "feudal" manner, in which the
obligations of the fighting men were limited
to a specific leader rather than to an
all-embracing cause or organization. The
modern European armies had a supremacy in
the field that only emulation could stop.
Gradually, by copying European weapon
manufacture and army organization, indigenous forces in parts of Africa and Asia were
better able to hold their own. By then,
however, the Europeans had established such
a clear advantage that it was already too late.

The growing disproportion of power
between Europe and the non-European
world can be seen as one of the prime causes
of the new imperialism of the late nineteenth century. Just as nature abhors a
vacuum, according to physics, so in international politics large, strong powers move
into areas regarded as weak. And it was
toward the end of the nineteenth century
that this disproportion of power became
particularly acute.

The international configuration likewise
seemed to favor empire building. From 1815
on, Western Europe experienced a hundred
years of internal peace, interrupted only by
short-term conflicts. This era of peace and
economic growth allowed the nations of
Europe to engage in overseas activities without fearing any immediate threat from their
neighbors. Overseas, many of the Asian and

African states with which Europe came in
contact were in the process of disintegrating.
In India the Mogul empire had collapsed
prior to British annexationism. The internal
disintegration of the Ottoman empire facili-
tated British, French, and Italian conquests
in North Africa and the Eastern Mediterranean. Chinese control over Indochina had
already slipped when the French began to
encroach on that area and, in Africa, many
of the powerful empires were also in eclipse.
European states in the nineteenth century
were motivated by nationalism, and also
possessed a strong sense of unity and purpose. While not passive in the face of
European onslaughts, Africans and Asians
lacked an equally powerful ideology to unite
them. Europeans were able to exploit old
divisions and animosities skillfully, and, by a
policy of divide and conquer, managed to
impose themselves on other cultures.

The advance of European power had
continued throughout the nineteenth century, but the tempo accelerated in the
1880s. Between 1880 and 1885 the French
annexed Tunisia, parts of the Western
Sudan, the Congo, Tahiti, and most of
Indochina. By 1890 the British had intensified existing activities in West Africa, expanded control over Southern and Central
Africa, encroached on the Malayan archi-
pelago, seized Egypt (1882), conquered
Burma (1886), and started on their East
African empire.

Three new powers which had not pre-
viously been involved in overseas activities
now entered the fray. The king of Belgium
established control over the Congo between
1879 and 1884; Italy gained territory on the
Horn of East Africa between 1883 and
1885; and in 1884 and 1885 Germany
staked out colonies in West, East, and Southern Africa and scattered islands in the South
Pacific. Areas not conquered in this spurt of
imperialism were mostly absorbed in the
1890s. The remainder were subjugated in the
decade and a half prior to World War I,
culminating in the French seizure of Morocco and the Italian attack on Libya in 1911.
By 1914 European expansion, as the result

of both earlier acquisitions and the "new imperialism," had affected most of the globe: only 15 percent of the earth's surface had never been ruled by Europeans.

The home scene changed during these years, too. While there had been several theorists of empire in earlier years, they now came into their own. Ideologies were unimportant as a cause of expansion, but they gave a martial tone to imperialism, defining the conquest of what they called the "lesser breeds of man" as Europe's destiny. Colonial societies flourished. Britain's Primrose League, which supported empire as well as other patriotic causes, boasted one million members. More singlemindedly, the Royal Colonial Institute represented over 3,000 members in the 1880s; and dozens of similar lobbies agitated for empire. In Germany several colonial societies were formed; the largest, the *Deutsche Kolonialverein,* founded in 1888, had over 30,000 members by 1902. Other German groups also supported imperialism: the Naval League (the *Deutscher Flottenverein*) was especially influential, with 5,000 local organizations and 650,000 members. French and Italian groups had smaller memberships but effectively focused the energies of influential bureaucrats and politicians who could implement policy. In general, these groups were founded after the first wave of imperialism and had little to do with the initial overseas expansion. Yet they encouraged and, in some crucial cases, determined expansionism subsequent to 1890.

An imperialist temper developed in the 1890s. Up to that time difficulties between European and non-European states had often been solved by diplomacy or other compromise. Beginning in the 1890s, however, Europeans increasingly chose to resort to force. Along with a penchant for violence went the cocky self-assurance and the racism exemplified by the British officer who announced, "I know nothing of politics, but I do know that if a nigger cheeks us, we must lick him." French Prime Minister Jules Ferry spoke of his nation's right and obligation "to civilize the inferior races," even if it meant the use of force. Each European state claimed to be particularly well-suited to play this "civilizing" role. Cecil Rhodes, the English empire-builder in Central Africa, declared, "We happen to be the best people in the world . . . and the more of the world we inhabit, the better it is for humanity." Imperialism became one of the most virulent expressions of the nationalism that had been developing in Europe.

Economics provided a further rationalization. Germany and England suffered depressions in the 1870s, as did France in the 1880s. In all three countries there were statesmen who believed that colonies would provide sure markets for European goods and thus cure the slump at home. In the 1870s and 1880s, there was a movement toward imposing protectionist tariffs. Fearing that they would be excluded from each other's markets, European states saw colonies as a haven for their goods. Strategic arguments were also made. In their competition with each other, European countries vied for advantageous locations as they anticipated future political and economic struggles. Statesmen pursued mirages and illusions of high profits, markets, and power.

Since the end of empires in the post-World War II era, the renewed interest in the history of imperialism has led to the publication of significant works that seek to illuminate the forces that produced the "new imperialism." Scholars disagree, citing contradictory evidence. The diversity of opinion mirrors the emphases and training of the scholars as well as the diversity of subjects studied. Thus, many of the essays in this volume reflect the specific conditions in a particular state at a particular moment. These studies are often fragmentary, highlighting only the policies of a single statesman, a single country, or a single instance of imperialism; the reader should be aware of this specialization in the literature in the last few years. At the same time, however, the studies show the complexity of motives and forces that led to Europe's dramatic subjugation of most of the globe in the past century.

Historians have produced two main generalizations to explain the many forces leading to imperialism. One interpretation stresses economics, while the other emphasizes politics. There is vigorous debate on the economics of empire. Godfrey Uzoigwe, the author of the first selection in this book, sees British policymakers in the 1880s as having been profoundly affected by economic concerns, such as the fear of a shrinking world market and the desire to create new outlets for British manufactures. His argument is somewhat different from that of Hobson, of course, who sees imperialism developing from the need to export excess capital. Instead, Uzoigwe sees imperialism as a result of a search for markets overseas. He also pays considerable attention to the perception of business leaders and publicists, insisting that their view of the economic situation, rather than necessarily the economic realities themselves, must be taken into account.

While modifying Hobson, Uzoigwe still presents a strong argument for economic motivation as being the basis of imperialism. David K. Fieldhouse presents one of the most detailed and sophisticated critiques of the Hobson-Lenin view of imperialism. Colonies, he shows, were hardly ever the destination of European capital exports; European investors preferred safer and higher-paying areas. Other economic benefits were also slim, and Fieldhouse demonstrates that the general unprofitability of empire was known. Yet empires continued to grow, thus revealing the existence of other, more important motives for imperialism.

Looking specifically at the French situation, Henri Brunschwig lends support to Fieldhouse's interpretation. The balance sheet of French imperialism, he reveals, was unfavorable. Although France's trade with its empire increased by 1914, this accounted for only about 15 percent of France's total foreign trade—certainly a fairly modest sum. If one also takes into account the small role that foreign trade played in France's overall economy, it becomes apparent that colonies were not very significant economically. Brunschwig sees French imperialism as having been motivated by the desire for glory to compensate for the national defeat at the

hands of Germany in 1870. To satisfy its thirst for great power status France embarked on empire and was willing to pay the costs.

The economic analysis of imperialism has at times been linked to a broader social interpretation, as in the selection by Hans-Ulrich Wehler, who argues that the domestic situation in Germany required Bismarck to carry out an imperialist policy abroad. Imperialism, Bismarck believed, would bridge the gap between agriculture and industry. At the same time it would create an outlet for trade and benefit the economy—which was in trouble as a result of the depression of the 1870s—and thus decrease class conflict between labor and capital inside Germany. Contented with its lot, labor would not revolt, and the social order would be preserved.

Jean-Louis Miège examines social factors, especially demography, to analyze the Italian experience. While he sees many factors leading to Italian expansionism abroad, Miège singles out the population problem as particularly salient. Fear of overpopulation at home and of the hemorrhaging of Italy's population to foreign lands led publicists and politicians to present imperialism as a solution. The acquisition of overseas possessions would provide a safety valve for the impoverished peasants of southern Italy; at the same time, it would ensure the peasants that if they left Italy, they could still live under Italian sovereignty, enjoying Italian culture, obeying Italian laws, and remaining a political and economic resource of the motherland.

These interpretations portray imperialism as being determined by economic and social pressures on the government. A more empirical and diversified interpretation is presented by Pierre Guillen. Examining the relationship between business and government in regard to imperialism, Guillen shows that this relationship was not always close: it varied according to the interests of the commercial groups and governments. Both groups were usually pragmatic and tried to use each other. In the final analysis Guillen seems to conclude that governments were in charge and used business for their own purposes. Empire may have paid off for a large group of businessmen and a select group of bankers, but they were rarely in a position to dictate government policy. Only when business and official interests coincided did governments embark on overseas conquests desired by businessmen.

In contrast to the economic analysis of imperialism is the political interpretation, which has many variants. Among the most prominent are those that see imperialism as a consequence of the development of European nationalism. Carlton Hayes offers this interpretation. He sees in the intellectual movements of nationalism and social Darwinism the seeds of imperialist policies. Politicians, playing to mass opinion, embraced jingoism at home and abroad. The conquest of distant lands was viewed as an assertion of national grandeur, which established claims for future greatness. Colonies were but pawns in the struggle among European nation states, imbued with nationalistic fervor.

In Hayes' view, imperialist statesmen both abetted and responded to public opinion. But some statesmen sought empire solely because of their own predilection for it, with no regard for public reaction. This was the case with King Leopold II of Belgium, who was avid to possess an empire and scoured the globe in search of a suitable colony. When he acquired the Congo in 1885, Leopold made it his personal fief; and it wasn't until 1908 that the Congo became a Belgian colony.

Political motivations had little to do with domestic issues or predilections of European statesmen, but were dictated instead by strategic considerations, argue Ronald Robinson and John Gallagher. Specifically, Robinson and Gallagher propose to interpret the partition of the greater part of Africa after 1882 by relating it to the Egyptian question. Britain occupied Egypt to safeguard the Suez Canal, a crucial link in sea communications with India. Worried lest European rivals establish themselves on the Nile and thus indirectly control the fate of Egypt, Britain advanced southward and, in the end, occupied the land between Cairo and the headwaters of the Nile in Uganda. The French, stung by the British occupation of Egypt (to which Frenchmen had laid special claim since Napoleon occupied it in 1798), were determined to force a British evacuation. They advanced toward Egypt from existing establishments, which explains the French move into Central Africa. The meeting of British and French forces at Fashoda, a small fort on the Nile, symbolized the clash of these two advancing imperialisms.

Both the economic and political interpretations claim that European imperialism developed from forces and motives originating in Europe itself. A number of theories, however, see European expansion as a result of forces unleashed in the non-European world. John Galbraith suggests that the incursions by neighboring peoples on existing colonies created a "turbulent frontier." To quell the disturbances, local officials went on raids and finally subjugated the neighboring peoples, thus enlarging the area of the colony. This enlarged possession, with its new boundaries, required further military expeditions to stabilize the recently acquired frontiers. Colonial officials, acting from both a zeal to establish order and from personal ambition, ignored specific orders from the home government or at least acquired new territories with no prior consultation with their governments.

Going one step further, Robinson suggests that non-European populations were an important ingredient in determining European expansion. These people had their own reasons for desiring collaboration with Europeans. When they did not desire this collaboration and were strong enough to resist it, Europeans failed to conquer.

The essays in this volume are selected from a rich and constantly growing literature. Controversial when it occurred, imperialism is still a subject of heated debate. It is hoped that this collection of essays will enlarge the reader's understanding of and sensitivity to one of the most significant trends of the late nineteenth century— European imperialism.

CONFLICT OF OPINION

I. ECONOMIC AND SOCIAL ORIGINS OF IMPERIALISM

"By 1895 most people of note believed that Britain's economic situation was not flourishing. There was a feeling that it must expand its commerce in unprotected markets or perish. . . . Imperialists saw the salvation in territorial expansion."

—G.N. UZOIGWE

"How far can it be said that the arguments put forward . . . make necessary a revision of the theory of 'imperialism' which derives from Hobson and Lenin? The general conclusion would seem to emerge that, as an historical interpretation of the expansion of European empires between 1870 and 1914, it is unacceptable. As an economic theory it is unsatisfactory because detailed investigations have shown that the alleged need of the European investor, monopolist, or individual capitalist, to find outlets for his surplus capital had little or nothing to do with the division of Africa and the Pacific."

—DAVID K. FIELDHOUSE

"The colonies did not supply French industry with a profitable monopoly. They could not have done so because French industry was not in a position to supply them. . . .The policy of expansion certainly cost France more than it brought in."

—HENRI BRUNSCHWIG

"Expansion was a part of the anti-cyclical economic policy intended as an antidote to the pessimism of the depression years and as an incentive which would stimulate business. The intention remained always the same: to take pressure off the home market by extending foreign trade, to stimulate an economic revival and thereby to reduce the strain on the social and political system."

—HANS-ULRICH WEHLER

"The statesmen who had unified Italy were particularly sensitive to the emigrants' great suffering. That Italy, barely reunited and restored, had to be abandoned, seemed at once cruel and antithetical to the *Risorgimento*. They wanted a national emigration to lands that had become Italian. This desire reinforced the 'imperialist themes,' latent in the unification movement."

—JEAN LOUIS MIÈGE

"Business interests were far from forming a homogenous interest group; the value they saw in overseas expansion and the form they thought it should take varied according to era and group . . . Business circles and government [were] . . . not inspired by the same motives."

—PIERRE GUILLEN

II. POLITICAL ORIGINS OF IMPERIALISM

"Basically the new imperialism was a nationalistic phenomenon. It followed hard upon the national wars which created an all-powerful Germany and a united Italy. . . .It expressed a resulting psychological reaction, an ardent desire to maintain or recover national prestige."

—CARLTON J.H. HAYES

"The colonial doctrine that Leopold II articulated at age twenty-five endured throughout his life. . . .All his policies were based on his doctrine; no particular circumstances led him to found colonies. He entered the race for empire simply because that was his program."

—J. STENGERS

"As they drew their new map of Africa by treaty, the statesmen of the great powers intended nothing so simple or so serious as the making of colonies there. . . .Those who presided over the partition saw it with a cold and detached view. It was not Africa itself which they saw; it was its bearing on their great concerns in Europe, the Mediterranean and the East. . . .From a European point of view, the partition treaties are monuments to the flights of imagination of which officials are capable, when dealing with a blank map of two-thirds of a continent."

—RONALD ROBINSON AND JOHN GALLAGHER

III. NON-EUROPEAN ORIGINS OF IMPERIALISM

"Governors charged with the maintenance of order could not ignore disorder beyond their borders, turbulence which pulled them toward expansion. . . .Despite the conviction on Downing Street that Britain should not intervene in the affairs of the native states, the governor by his reports and by his actions created the conditions which forced the Home Government to a contrary policy."

—JOHN S. GALBRAITH

"From beginning to end imperialism was a product of interaction between European and extra-European politics. European economic and strategic expansion took imperial form when these two components operated at cross-purposes with the third and non-European component—that of indigenous collaboration and resistance. . . .Without indigenous collaboration, when the time came for it, Europeans [could not] have conquered and ruled their non-European empires."

—RONALD ROBINSON

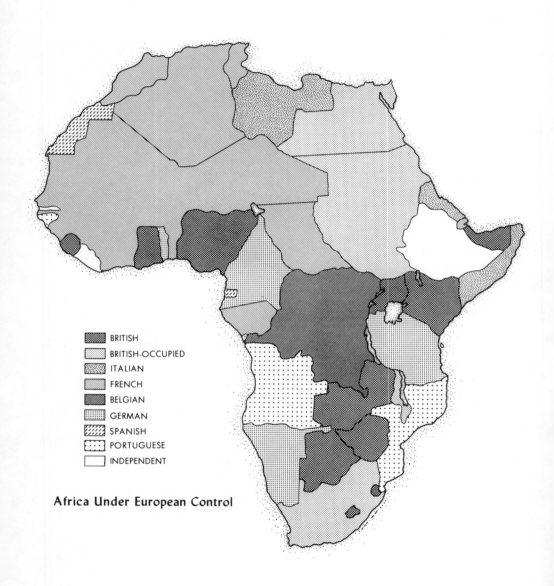

BRITISH
BRITISH-OCCUPIED
ITALIAN
FRENCH
BELGIAN
GERMAN
SPANISH
PORTUGUESE
INDEPENDENT

Africa Under European Control

Maps courtesy of John Hollingsworth,
Indiana University.

Colonial Africa

(with place names mentioned in text)

MOROCCO

TUNISIA
Tunis
Tripoli

ALGERIA

LIBYA

EGYPT

S A H A R A   D E S E R T

Nile R.

RED SEA

Tel el-Kebir Sta.
Alexandria
Cairo
Suez Canal

WESTERN   SUDAN

Timbuktu

Senegal R.

GAMBIA
SENEGAL
GUINEA
FUTA

Niger R.

DAHOMEY
Lagos

NIGERIA

IVORY COAST

GERMAN WEST AFRICA

LAKE CHAD

DARFUR

SUDAN

Wadi Halfa
Dongola
Khartum
Adowa

Bahr al Ghazal
Fashoda
Sobat R.

Addis Ababa

ETHIOPIA

ITALIAN SOMALILAND

UBANGUI SHARI

CAMEROONS

GABUN

Brazzaville

CONGO

Congo R.

Kilo Mota

UGANDA

LAKE VICTORIA NYANZA

KASAI

KATANGA

GERMAN EAST AFRICA

Mombasa
Zanzibar

TANGANYIKA

NYASA-LAND

LAKE NYASA

NORTHERN RHODESIA

Zambezi R.

SOUTHERN RHODESIA

SOUTHWEST AFRICA

BECHUANA-LAND

TRANSVAAL

GRIQUALAND

NATAL

BASUTOLAND

Orange R.

SOUTH AFRICA

Gt. Fish R.
Keis Kamma R.

The Cape

SIMON'S BAY

MADAGASCAR

0	400	800 Miles
0	400	800	1200 Kilometers

I. ECONOMIC AND SOCIAL ORIGINS OF IMPERIALISM

Godfrey N. Uzoigwe

COMMERCE AND EMPIRE

Professor Godfrey N. Uzoigwe (1938-   ), Nigerian-born and British-educated, is the author of several books on African history and is a professor of history at the University of Michigan. Examining British economic developments in the latter part of the nineteenth century, he concludes that British commentators and statesmen were seriously concerned with the economic conditions and prospects of Britain. Many saw imperialism as a solution to Britain's dilemmas. In this selection, Uzoigwe emphasizes both the economic realities and the perception of them by British contemporaries.

A. New British Markets and Foreign Competition

"YOU CANNOT get them to talk of politics so long as they are well employed," wrote William Matthews in 1883. Economic factors, social conditions, and politics are delicately connected. The historian who discusses the one in isolation of the others does so at his peril. To dismiss economic motivations as an unimportant factor in imperial expansion is as delusive as to argue that these motivations alone were the only justification for imperialism. The most surprising thing about the theory of economic imperialism or of any of the current theories, is its failure to take into consideration what the participants said, or implied, motivated their actions. What the opponents of economic imperialism are doing, in effect, is to use present-day knowledge in interpreting what happened in the past and under different circumstances. The reverse should be the case. Instead of posing the question: Was Africa worth having?, we should ask: Did contemporaries believe that it was worth having? And if so, why?

"New markets! New markets!," wrote Frederick Greenwood, "is the constant cry of our captains of industry and merchant princes, and it is well that to them the ear of government should willingly incline. It ought to do so, and it does." By new markets he meant primarily those regions yet unacquired by any European power, for example, western China, Tibet, and tropical Africa. The argument was that the acquisition of these markets—which implied the control of the countries themselves—would nullify the effects of hostile tariffs by creating an open door to world trade, and to

Reprinted with permission from G. N. Uzoigwe, *Britain and the Conquest of Africa: The Age of Salisbury* (Ann Arbor: University of Michigan Press, 1974), pp. 24-25, 27-29, 34-35, 37. Copyright ©1974 by the University of Michigan.

British trade in particular, thereby helping to cure its economic ills. This argument was given more weight by the industrial unrest and unemployment which occurred in the early nineties. In 1891 Salisbury advocated African expansion as indispensable to British prosperity, employment, and world power. The British Chamber of Commerce declared: "There is practically no middle course for this country, between a reversal of free-trade policy to which it is pledged, on the one hand, and a prudent but continuous territorial expansion for the creation of new markets." On subsequent occasions Salisbury, Rosebery, and Chamberlain endorsed this view. In 1895 Salisbury warned that "at a period when the other outlets for the commercial energies of our countrymen were being gradually closed by the enormous growth of protectionist doctrines amongst other States, it was our business in all these new countries to smooth the path of British enterprise and to facilitate the application of British capital."

In an important speech at Bradford in the following May, he dwelt once more on the same theme. He spoke of "the dreary period of general depression and difficulty and distress through which we have passed for the last few years"; and he blamed it on hostile tariffs. To avoid repetition of such depression, he [Salisbury] implored his audience "to make our way not only in the civilized, but in the uncivilized, markets of the world.". . .

In November 1896 Chamberlain asserted that "commerce is the greatest of all political interests. . . .All the great offices of State are occupied with commercial affairs."

The Times, too, published an article entitled "The Commercial Value of Africa." It showed that the immediate commercial value of tropical Africa was not startling, but admitted that given suitable conditions necessary for commercial development, the situation would drastically change. The same was true of India which, under British guidance, was not more valuable commercially than the whole of Africa. It concluded:

The fact is that up to within the past few years Africa has hardly been needed by the rest of the world except as a slave market. But her turn has come, and the need for her cooperation in the general economy of the world will become greater and greater as population increases, as industry expands, as commerce develops, as States grow ambitious, as civilization spreads. It is a discreditable anomaly that at this advanced stage in the progress of the race nearly a whole continent should still be given over to savagery. . . .We now take only what is most easily reached.

In September *The Times* emphasized the dangers of foreign competition and renewed Salisbury's earlier call. "Some countries in which we once had a monopoly of the supply," it lamented, "have been learning of late to manufacture of themselves, and have become more or less independent of us. In others, the strain is caused by the competition of foreign traders, who contrive to draw to themselves no small share of business which we have been in the habit of considering our own." A year later, it wondered whether British merchants ever bothered to read the Blue Books published for their benefit. "If the supremacy of British commerce is to be preserved," it warned, "our traders must bestir themselves betimes." Indeed, *The Times* proudly acknowledged that British imperialism was economic. . . . The *Pall Mall Gazette* affirmed that Britain desired Africa primarily for its trading needs, and even felt a tinge of pride in saying so. It wrote:

Nor have we gone to the equatorial regions from religious or humanitarian motives. Missionaries and philanthropists, indeed, complain sometimes that their work is hampered by Downing Street regulations. Still less have we sought out the African in order to endow him with the vices (and virtues) of Western civilization.

Writing many years afterwards, Lugard more or less endorsed these views. He argued that the trade of British tropical Africa was "more than double that of India per head of population, and more than a quarter of its total volume, and is equal per head to that of Japan." Chamberlain was said to have been interested in Nigeria "because it produced palm oil." And in 1898 Benjamin Kidd published a series of articles in which he produced statistics—the exact source of which he did not indicate—to advertise the growing importance of tropical commerce. He argued "that our own trade with the tropics is already a very large proportion of our total commerce." He showed that, taking British trade with *all* her colonies and dependencies, trade with her tropical empire considerably exceeded her trade with non-tropical colonies and dependencies, including Canada, the Cape, Natal, New Zealand, and Australia, Queensland excepted. Again, taking the English-speaking world as a whole, but excluding their trade within their own frontiers, their trade with the tropics accounted for 38 percent of their total trade with the rest of the world. Also the United States trade with the tropics accounted for 65 percent of her total trade with the rest of the world. And the combined United Kingdom and United States trade with the tropics averaged 44 percent of their total trade with the rest of the world outside English-speaking countries. Kidd asked his readers to heed the Frenchman who said: "Colonization is for France a question of life and death—either France must become a great African power or she will be in a century or two but a secondary European power; she will count in the world scarcely more than Greece or Rumania counts in Europe." And Kidd himself prophesied that the struggle for tropical trade would be "the permanent underlying fact in the foreign relations of the Western nations in the twentieth century" because of their dependence on tropical products and the mutual profitability of trade.

B. The Decline of Britain's Commercial Supremacy

Were these fears justified? Indeed they were; but contemporaries tended to exaggerate the imminence of Britain's economic collapse. Between 1846 and 1872 British trade "increased greatly while that of other countries, comparatively speaking, remained at best stationary." And from 1860 to about 1872 Britain had perhaps the fastest rate of economic growth in the world. After 1875 the rate slowed down considerably, and the trend continued to about 1914. By the mid-eighties the situation had become one of considerable concern to the government, and led to a series of official inquiries. In 1895 farmers from all over the country were driven by the continuing agricultural depression to urge Salisbury to resort to protection, but he refused to comply. There was also a gradual price decline which set in about 1873 and lasted to about 1894. From then to the end of the century there was gradual improvement. But of greater consequence was the rising competition of other powers and their adoption of protective tariffs injurious to England's foreign trade, which constituted "one of the most powerful influences on the state of the British economy." The rate of growth of English exports after 1875 declined considerably until the close of the century, when its performance began to be "comparable to that of the mid-Victorian years." The result was that the comfortable commercial supremacy which England had maintained up to about 1872 began gradually to be reversed. It was not that the country was stagnating as such, but that she was gradually being equalled, and in certain aspects surpassed, by the United States, Germany and, to a negligible extent, France. But, to take some concrete examples: In 1881 British coal miners numbered 382,000 and exported £8 million worth of coal; in 1901 the number had increased to 644,000, and coal exports had soared to £38 million. This sounds impressive until it is compared with America's performance, which by 1900 had outstripped England. And the impact of America's emergence as a large-scale world exporter of manufactures caused alarm in England. In the important iron and steel industry, England had, by 1900, been pushed from first to third position behind Germany and the United States. In 1871 England produced just over 6½ million tons of pig iron; Germany and the United States produced 1½ million each. In 1902 England increased its production by only 2 million, to 8½ million; Germany stood at par with it, while the United States, which had already overtaken it in 1886, now produced over 17 million tons. . . .

While America, Germany, and France maintained some sort of reasonable equilibrium between exports and imports, British imports far outstripped its exports. In other words, Britain was living beyond its means and had a balance of payments crisis especially between 1890 and 1902. Around 1872 Britain earned just over £250 million from its total exports; its imports amounted to just over £350 million. By 1895 its total exports fell to just over £200 million, while its imports stood at just over £400 million, i.e., almost double the exports. The period 1890-95 was a particularly bad one for British trade. Exports took a disastrous dive, while imports doubled exports. This gave rise to the cry for new markets. Between 1895 and 1902 there was a steady recovery, with exports reaching an all-time high of around £275 million in 1900; but this was vitiated by a phenomenal rise in imports to around £525 million in 1900. Again, the period 1895-1900 coincided with the extension and consolidation of Britain's imperial hold in Africa.

Evidently, those who cried for new markets had every reason to be alarmed. It can, of course, be argued that since the cry for new markets only became loud in the 1890s when Africa had practically been partitioned, it was a mere rationalization after the event. It must be pointed out, however, that those in authority were not unaware of Britain's economic difficulties in the 1880s. That this consideration may have driven them to participate in the greatest international shareout in world history cannot be ruled out. Rosebery's summary of the partition as pegging out claims for futurity explains a great deal about this. Moreover, the fact that the rationalization itself should take a strong economic orientation is in itself significant. Indeed Africa may have been partitioned in the 1880s, but this was only on paper. The real partition took place in the 1890s with effective occupation. A more interesting question, however, is whether these unprotected markets, after

acquisition, fulfilled the expectations held out for them. This is open to debate. Some contemporaries thought they did; others dissented. But no one disagreed that British commerce was not flourishing. Optimists, like Kidd, placed a high store on tropical commerce. Lord Masham was convinced that trade followed the flag; as also was *The Times,* though in regard to Africa, it believed that the fruits of the annexations belonged to the future. Writing in 1904, Maxse was emboldened to ask:

What would be the attitude of the discredited apostle [Cobden] were he with us today? He would be compelled by facts to recognize, little Englander though he was, that the Empire and the Empire alone had saved this island from industrial collapse by taking in ever-increasing quantities the goods rejected elsewhere. Possibly Cobden might be sufficiently sagacious to pocket his political prejudices in the interests of his economic faith, and turn his remarkable energies to the development of the Colonial market. . . .

Our problem, in a word, is to recreate the Empire which Chatham founded and which Cobden failed to lose.

Was Maxse's optimism founded? In 1872 British exports to its possessions amounted to £60 million; in 1902 they soared to £109 million. Its export trade with all Europe was £108 million in 1872; in 1902 it was £96½ million. With the United States it was £40,700,000 in 1872 and £27,800,000 in 1902. "Thus the decrease of 11½ millions in our European trade," wrote Marston, "and of 13 millions in our trade with the United States, had been wiped out by an increase of 49 millions with British possession." In other words, it means that "in 1902 we sent as great a value of goods to our colonies as we did to Germany, Holland, the United States, South America, Mexico, France, Russia, China, Turkey, and Persia combined.". . .

It is clear that by 1895 most people of note believed that Britain's economic situation was not flourishing. There was a feeling that it must expand its commerce in unprotected markets or perish. "Our natural inheritance," wrote Kidd, "is the trade of the world." He advocated the maintenance of a navy stronger than those of the other nations put together to protect this trade against competition. Campbell-Bannerman pointed out that "12 million of our people are underfed, and on the verge of hunger." The Cobden club admitted that "our overseas trade has increased less rapidly than our population." Others longed for the return of "the great Victorian boom," and "the good years"; but as a shrewd observer had recently remarked, millions still lived "below the poverty line" during those so-called years of prosperity. If, then, all shades of opinion wanted the extension of British commerce, how could this be achieved? In this they disagreed. Imperialists saw the salvation in territorial expansion.

David K. Fieldhouse

ECONOMIC EXPLANATIONS RECONSIDERED

David K. Fieldhouse (1925-   ) is Beit Lecturer in the History of the Commonwealth at Oxford and a Fellow of Nuffield College, Oxford. He is the author of several works on imperialism, including *Colonial Empires* (1966) and *Economics and Empire* (1973). In this selection Fieldhouse gives a survey of the economic interpretation of imperialism and offers a detailed critique. No one can afford to ignore the criticisms he provides at both the general and specific levels of the economic interpretation.

I T IS NOW nearly sixty years since J. A. Hobson published *Imperialism: A Study,* and thereby gave the word the connotation it still generally carries. His conception of the nature of "imperialism" has, indeed, been almost universally accepted and, partly through the expository literature it has generated, may be said to have exercised a significant historical influence. Yet, for all its success, Hobson's argument has always been extremely vulnerable to criticism: and it is therefore surprising that those historians and economists who have argued effectively that his analysis is basically unsound should have received so little attention. The aim of the present article is to draw together some of the more important arguments that have been put forward for and against his thesis, and to suggest that, on balance, the no's have it.

Hobson's own claim to importance and originality lies simply in his having seduced British and, subsequently, world opinion to accept his own special definition of the word imperialism. Professor Koebner has already examined the various meanings given to the

Reprinted with permission from D. K. Fieldhouse, "Imperialism, An Historiographical Revision," in *Economic History Review*, 2nd ser. XIV (1961), pp. 187-193, 195-196, 199-209.

word before 1902. He has suggested that, as used in England, it had two general connotations in the 1890s, both of which were morally neutral. In one sense, it was being used of those who wished to prevent the existing British settlement colonies from seceding and becoming independent states, and was therefore a conservative factor. In another and increasingly common sense, it was being used to indicate an expansionist and "forward" attitude towards problems connected with the future control of the "uncivilized" parts of the world, such as Africa, the Middle East and the Pacific. Salisbury was, in this sense, regarded as an imperialist in accepting the need for Britain to share in the partition of East Africa. Gladstone, in opposing the acquisition of Uganda, was emphatically anti-imperialist, even though he had acquiesced in the need to gain some control over Egypt in 1882. In the eyes of the anti-imperialists the sin of expansionism lay in the waste of money entailed on armaments, in the cost of colonial governments, and in the danger of international conflicts over intrinsically unimportant territories which would be wiser to leave alone. As a rule no worse motive was attributed to the imperialists than "jingoism" or excessive concern with Britain's position as a great power.

But between 1896 and 1902 imperialism, as a word, began to lose its innocence. Koebner has shown that events in South Africa, and particularly the Jameson Raid, gave rise to a suspicion that, here at least, the expansive urge was motivated by something other than a concern for national greatness by what Harcourt called "stock-jobbing imperialism"—based on the interests of financiers. This was, of course, a special case; and a distinction remained between an honest, even if misguided, imperialism, and the debased variety to be seen on the Rand. Yet the idea now gained ground that South Africa might not, after all, be a special case, but might exhibit in an extreme form a factor inherent in all expansionism. By 1900 radical opinion had moved so far in this direction that the Fifth International So-

cialist Congress, taught probably by its English delegation, could resolve

...que le développement du capitalisme mène fatalement à l'expansion coloniale. . .: que la politique coloniale de la bourgeoisie n'a d'autre but que d'élargir les profits de la classe capitaliste et le maintien du système capitaliste. [The development of capitalism inevitably leads to colonial expansion. . .; the colonial policy of the possessing classes has no other goal than increasing the profits of the capitalist class and the preservation of the capitalist system.]

Here, in a nutshell, was Hobson's doctrine of "imperialism." But it remained to be seen whether such a dogmatic interpretation would ever command a wide support; and it was essentially his achievement to ensure that, in his own non-Marxist form, it should become the generally accepted theory.

Hobson's *Imperialism* therefore came out at a time when British public opinion, disillusioned by the Boer War, was already profoundly suspicious about the motives behind recent imperial expansion. It was, in fact, a pamphlet for the times, rather than a serious study of the subject; and, like all pamphlets that achieve influence, it owed much of its success to the fact that it expressed a current idea with peculiar clarity, force and conviction. It arose immediately out of Hobson's visit to South Africa during the war, and derived from reports [which] he sent back to *The Speaker,* [and] which were published as a book in 1900 as *The War in South Africa, Its Causes and Effects.* Yet, paradoxically, Hobson was not primarily concerned with imperial problems: and *Imperialism* can only be properly understood on the basis that his interest, then and throughout his life, was with the social and economic problems of Britain. In a sense, this book was primarily a vehicle for publicizing the theory of "underconsumption," which he regarded as his main intellectual achievement, and which he expressed more fully in *The Evolution of Modern Capitalism,* and other works. In brief, the theory, which was an alternative to the Marxist concept of surplus value as an explanation of poverty, saw excessive investment by the capitalist, with it concomitant of under-consumption by the wage-earner, as the root cause of concurrent slumps, of low interest rates, and of permanent under-employment. Hobson thought there were only two answers to this problem. The correct one—which would also be the answer to the "condition of England question"—was to increase the buying power of the workers by giving them a higher share of the profits of industry. The wrong one, which was no answer to the social question, was to invest the surplus capital overseas, where it could earn a high interest rate and thus sustain domestic rates of interest, without bene-fiting the British worker. And this, he held, was what Britain had been doing since at least the middle of the nineteenth century.

To this point the economic theory, though highly vulnerable, has no apparent relevance to the phenomenon of overseas expansion, that is, to imperialism. The key to Hobson's theory of imperialism lies in the connection he makes between the two.

Overproduction in the sense of an excessive manu-facturing plant, and surplus capital which could not find sound investments within the country, forced Great Britain, Germany, Holland, [and] France to place larger and larger portions of their economic resources outside the area of their present political domain, and then stimulate a policy of political expansion so as to take in the areas.

Thus "imperialism," in the special sense used by Hobson, is an external symptom of a social malady in the metropolitan countries. Without this domestic pressure for invest-ment overseas, there would be no effective impulse towards the acquisition of new colonies. Conversely, without colonies, capital would lack an outlet, and domestic rates of interest would sink. Thus the need to export capital and to make it politically secure overseas was what Mr. John Strachey has recently called the "prime mover for the modern imperialist process." And "imperial-ism," on this assumption, is not variously sound or stock-jobbing; but, without excep-tion, results from the special economic interests of the capitalist, and is therefore "economic imperialism."

It is not proposed at this stage to examine Hobson's theory in detail: but some comment must be made on the logical value of the argument he uses to demonstrate the historical truth of this hypothesis. Does he, in fact, supply any evidence to support the claim that colonies were the product of a demand either for new investment oppor-tunities, or for security for existing invest-ments? He begins with a straightforward account of the expansion of the European empires since 1870, printing a list of terri-tories acquired by Britain which Lenin, and later Mr. Strachey, have reproduced. Then, in chapter two, he demonstrates that the expansion of the British empire had been of little apparent value to British trade; that trade with these recent acquisitions was the least valuable part of intra-imperial trade; and that British trade with all colonies was declining in relation to trade with the rest of the world. Clearly then, imperialism was not good for trade. Nor was it good for emigra-tion (which, in any case, he thought un-necessary), since these new tropical colonies were quite unsuited to white settlement. And his conclusion was that

The Imperialism of the last six decades is clearly condemned as a business policy, in that at enor-mous expense it has procured a small, bad, unsafe increase of markets, and has jeopardized the entire wealth of the nation in arousing the strong resentment of other nations.

How then can a motive be found for this imperial expansion? The motive is to be seen if, alongside the list of territorial acquisi-tions, is placed a table showing the increase of British overseas investments in the same period. It then becomes obvious that, during the period in which British possessions had increased by 4,754 m. square miles and by a population of 88 millions, British overseas investments had also increased enor-mously—from £144 m. to £1698 m. between 1862 and 1893 alone. Could there be any doubt that the two sets of figures were intimately connected as cause and effect? Hobson had no doubts about it: "It is not too much to say that the modern foreign policy of Great Britain has been primarily a struggle for profitable markets of investment."

But it is immediately apparent that Hobson had in no sense proved that there was any connection between the investments made overseas and the territory acquired contemporaneously. His table of investments makes no differentiation between the areas in which investment had taken place, beyond such classifications as "Foreign," "Colonial," "U.S.A." and "Various," and, in fact, he assumes quite arbitrarily that the new colonies had attracted a high proportion of the investment called "Foreign" (i.e. before they were annexed) or "Colonial" (subsequent to annexation). This, it will be suggested below, is a basic fault of his theory of imperialism. Indeed, to put the case bluntly, Hobson performed an intellectual conjuring trick. Convinced of the essential truth of his economic theory, he deceived the eye by the speed of his hand, creating the illusion that, of the two sets of statistics he held up, one was the cause of the other.

It is not possible here to consider the rest of Hobson's *Imperialism,* interesting though it is in relation to related controversies over protection, tariff reform and imperial unity. But two additional points in his main argument must be mentioned because they were intrinsic to his definition of the origins and nature of imperialist expansion.

The first of these concerns the relationship between the financial interest and other imperialists, and is therefore crucial to his theory. He was aware that, contrary to his argument, the obvious driving force of British expansion since 1870 appeared to lie in the explorers, missionaries, engineers, patriotic pressure groups, and empire-minded politicians, all of whom had evident influence and had demonstrable interests, other than those of investment, in territorial acquisitions. And he was equally aware that if the impulse to expansion could be satisfactorily explained in the old-fashioned terms of their idealism, their ambition, or their concern with the status of Britain as a world power, rather than in terms of the self-interest of the capitalist, his own central

thesis would collapse. It was therefore necessary that these men—the Lugards, the Milners, the Johnstons, and the Roseberys—should be shown to be mere puppets—the tools of imperialism rather than its authors. Hobson did this by falling back on what may be called the "faceless men" gambit:

Finance manipulates the patriotic forces which politicians, soldiers, philanthropists, and traders generate; the enthusiasm for expansion which issues from these sources, though strong and genuine, is irregular and blind; the financial interest has those qualities of concentration and clear-sighted calculation which are needed to set Imperialism to work. An ambitious statesman, a frontier soldier, an over-zealous missionary, a pushing trader, may suggest or even initiate a step of imperial expansion, may assist in educating patriotic public opinion to the urgent need of some fresh advance, but the final determination rests with the financial power.

In this ingenious way Hobson inverted the apparent relationship between the obvious imperialists and the investor. Instead of the financier being induced to invest in new possessions, with more or less enthusiasm, once political control had been imposed for other reasons, he becomes the essential influence in the takeover itself. Investment no longer follows the flag: it decides where it is profitable to plant it, and tells the government whether it is to follow the advice of men of action or of ideas in each particular case. Thus, imperialism can never be interpreted as the spontaneous expression of the idealism, the chauvinism or the mere energy of a nation. In its practical form it is the expression of the special interests of the financier behind the scenes, who decides whether it is worth his while to allow a dream to become a reality, and who alone will reap the benefits.

This assumption, which has been adopted by most subsequent supporters of Hobson's thesis, will be examined later.

The other essential point in the theory of imperialism is the suggestion that the possession of colonies by individual capitalist states results automatically in the exploitation of the indigenous peoples of Africa and Asia. In his long chapter "Imperialism and the Lower Races," which is in many ways one of the most undogmatic and constructive parts of the book, Hobson argued that exploitation, whether by appropriation of land or by the use of cheap labor—forced or nominally free—in mines, farms and factories, had been a general feature of the colonies of all the European powers. Hobson, in the British humanitarian tradition, thought such exploitation to be both wrong and inexpedient. Economic development was good for undeveloped colonies and for the world as a whole. The danger lay in allowing the financiers to use the political power of the imperial authority for their own purposes; and the solution was for international control of colonies—the germ of the later mandate concept—and patience in allowing normal economic forces to give the natives an inducement to work freely in European enterprises. Sensible as his general attitude was, it is clear that Hobson had thus included in imperialism the suggestion that countries possessing colonies were almost certain to exploit them in their own interests; and this argument was to become a staple of later critics of colonialism.

The theory of imperialism as it developed after the publication of Hobson's *Study* continued to be founded on the three main concepts outlined above. Yet in examining its historiography, it is clear that it was Lenin, writing in 1916, rather than Hobson himself, who gave imperialism its dogmatic coherence and much of its eventual influence. It is therefore necessary to consider briefly the extent to which Lenin modified Hobson's ideas.

The greatest difference lies in the first and most important part of the argument; that is, in the nature of the internal pressure in the capitalist countries which forces them to expand their colonial possessions. Hobson has explained this pressure in terms of underconsumption: but Lenin naturally had a more orthodox theory to hand. Capitalism as a system was approaching the apocalypse Marx had foretold. Competitive capitalism had, in the late nineteenth century, been replaced by "monopoly capitalism," with its characteristic agencies, the cartels, trusts and tariffs. It was no longer dynamic, but anxious only to maintain its profit margins by more intensive exploitation of limited and protected markets. Moreover, the "finance-capitalists"—the banks and trusts—who now largely controlled capital itself, found that under monopoly conditions it was more profitable to employ surplus capital abroad than in domestic industry. At home it could only increase production, lower prices, and raise wages. Abroad it could give a high interest return without any of these consequences. But, to gain the highest return from overseas investment it was desirable to have some political control over the territory in which the investment was made. This might be in the limited form of a "semi-colony," such as the Argentine. But only in the colony proper could really comprehensive economic and political controls be imposed which would give investments their highest return. The result had been the competition between the great powers to acquire new colonies after 1870, which would continue until the whole uncivilized world had come under imperial rule. Then would follow the inter-imperial wars for the redivision of the empires, leading to proletarian revolutions in the imperialist states, the creation of socialist states, and so, automatically, to the end of imperialism.

How much, then, does Lenin's explanation of the force behind imperialism differ from that of Hobson? Fundamentally, only in this: that, whereas Hobson used his theory as evidence that social-democratic reform at home was necessary and possible to eliminate the evil of underconsumption and therefore make imperialism unnecessary, Lenin made imperialism the definition of an inherent and unavoidable stage in the growth of capitalist society which could not be "reformed." Hobson was a doctor prescribing a remedy, Lenin a prophet forecasting catastrophe. But, while they disagreed as to the precise causes, both maintained that there existed in the capitalist countries a tremendous pressure for overseas investment, and that this was the main factor in producing imperialist expansion after 1870. . . .

The central feature of the theory of imperialism, by which it must stand or fall, is the assertion that the empires built up after 1870 were not an option but a necessity for the economically advanced states of Europe and America: that these capitalist societies, because of their surplus of domestically-produced capital, were forced to export capital to the underdeveloped regions of the world; and that it was only this investment—prospective or existing—that supplied a motive for the acquisition of new colonies.

Faced with this theory, the historian who does not take its truth for granted is likely to be skeptical on at least three main grounds. First, his instinct is to distrust all-embracing historical formulas which, like the concept of the rise of the middle class, seek to explain complex developments in terms of a single dominant influence. Again, he is likely to suspect an argument that isolates the imperial expansion of the period after 1870 from all earlier imperial developments if only because he is aware of so many elements of continuity in the history of overseas empires over the past few centuries. But, above all, he must be aware that the theory simply does not appear to fit the facts of the post-1870 period as he knows them. Looking, for example, at Hobson's list of territories acquired by Britain after 1870, it seems, at first sight at least, difficult to believe that any considerable part of them were annexed either because British capitalists had already invested much of their surplus capital there, or because they regarded them as fields for essential future investment. In some cases, perhaps, it seems that a *prima facie* case could be made out on these lines—for Egypt, the Transvaal and Rhodesia, to take Hobson's three main examples. But even in these, further consideration must arouse doubts. Surely the strategic importance of the Suez Canal was as good a reason for controlling Egypt in 1882 as the preservation of the interests of the bond holders in the Canal Company. Was it really necessary, on purely economic grounds, to annex the Transvaal in 1899 when the British mine-owners were making

vast fortunes under Kruger's government, and had shown themselves so divided over the question of the Jameson Raid and the independence of the Republic? Again, granted that Rhodes and the British South Africa Company had excellent economic reasons for wanting British control over Rhodesia, was their anxiety really due to the pressure of British funds waiting for investment opportunity?

Doubts such as these concerning even the key examples chosen by Hobson inevitably stimulate further examination of his list: and this makes it clear that not even a *prima facie* case could be made out for most of the territories he includes. To take a random selection, it would surely be ludicrous to suggest that Fiji, British New Guinea or Upper Burma were annexed in order to protect large British investments, or even as a field for subsequent investment. In each case secular explanations seem fully to account for their annexation: the chaotic condition of a mixed society in the Pacific, the fears of Australia for her military security, and the frontier problems of India. And even where, as in Malaya, large capital investment did take place after annexation, the time factor must be considered. Were the British investor and the government really so alert to the possible future need for fields for investment? Or did annexation in fact take place for quite other reasons, being followed by investment when new conditions and new possibilities arose which were then totally unforeseen. . .?

Hobson was entirely wrong in assuming that any large proportion of British overseas investment went to those undeveloped parts of Africa and Asia which were annexed during the imperialist grab after 1870. As Professor Nurkse has remarked of Hobson:

Had he tried to do what he did for trade, that is, to show the geographical distribution of overseas investment, he would have found that British capital tended to bypass the primitive tropical economies and flowed mainly to the regions of recent settlement outside as well as inside the British Empire.

And the figures published by Paish in 1911 demonstrate this conclusively. The bulk of

British investment then lay in the United States, £688 m.; South America, £587 m.; Canada, £372 m.; Australasia, £380 m.; India and Ceylon, £365 m.; and South Africa, £351 m. By contrast, West Africa had received only £29 m., the Straits and Malay States £22 m., and the remaining British possessions £33 m. These last were, of course, by no means negligible amounts, and indicate clearly that in some at least of the tropical dependencies which had been recently acquired, British finance was finding scope for profit and investment. But this does not make Hobson's thesis any more valid. The sums invested in these tropical areas, whether newly annexed or not, were quite marginal to the total overseas investment, and continued to be relatively very small in the years immediately before 1911. Hence, to maintain that Britain had found it necessary to acquire these territories because of an urgent need for new fields for investment is simply unrealistic; and with the rejection of this hypothesis, so ingeniously conjured up by Hobson, the whole basis of his theory that imperialism was the product of economic necessity collapses.

But to suggest that Hobson and Lenin were mistaken in thinking that the need to export capital from Europe after 1870 was so intense that it made the colonization of most of Africa and the Pacific necessary as fields for investment is merely to throw the question open again. The essential problem remains: On what other grounds is it possible to explain this sudden expansion of European possessions, whose motive force is called imperialism?

For the historian it is natural to look for an explanation of these developments which is not based on *a priori* reasoning, does not claim to be a comprehensive formula, and is not out of line with long-term historical developments. It would, of course, be unreasonable to expect to find in the late nineteenth century any precise repetition of earlier patterns of imperial expansion; at the same time it would seem reasonable to look carefully for evidence of continuity of motive and policy with earlier periods before falling back on the conclusion that events after 1870 were unique.

Looking broadly over the four centuries since the early Portuguese discoveries, it may be said that, although European motives for acquiring colonies were extremely complex, they fell into two general categories. First was the specifically economic motive, whose aim was to create a lucrative trade for the metropolitan country. Its typical expression was the trading base or factory, secured by some form of agreement with the local ruler: but, where no commodities already existed for trade, it could result in territorial possessions, like the sugar islands of the Caribbean, or the spice islands of the East; the fur-producing parts of North America, and the silver mines of Peru. The export of capital played no significant part in this economic activity, for Europe had little surplus capital before the nineteenth century, and investment was restricted to the immediate needs of trade itself, of the mines, sugar estates, etc.

By contrast, it is clear that from the earliest days of European expansion the margin between economic and other motives was small, and that many colonies were rather the product of political and military rivalries than of the desire for profit. The mercantile practices followed by all European states were as much concerned with national power as with economic advantage, and tended, as Adam Smith pointed out, to subordinate opulence to the needs of security. Indeed, by the eighteenth century, imperial policies had come to be largely a reflection of European power politics: and the struggle for territorial supremacy in America, India and the strategic bases on the route to the East were the outcome of political rather than of strictly economic competition. Britain's decision to retain Canada rather than Guadaloupe in 1763 may perhaps stand as an example of preference given to a colony offering mainly military security and prestige over one whose value was purely economic.

If, then, a general view of pre-nineteenth-century imperial policies shows the complexity of its aims—made still more complicated in the early nineteenth century by the important new element of humanitarianism—it must seem surprising that Hobson should have interpreted post-1870 imperialism in narrowly economic terms, and have ignored the possibility that strictly political impulses may once again have been of major importance. The reason would seem to be that the evolution of imperial practices since about 1815 appeared, at the end of the century, to have constituted a clear break with earlier methods; to have made both the economic and the political criteria of earlier times irrelevant; and thus to have made comparison pointless. With the independence of almost all the American colonies, and the subsequent adoption by Britain—the chief remaining colonial power —of the practices of free trade, the possession of colonies no longer offered any positive economic advantage. The colonial trades were now open to all; bullion-hunting became the function of the individual prospector; and emigration, although it led to new British colonies in Australasia, flowed more naturally into the existing states of the new world. On the political side also, colonies had ceased to play an important part in diplomacy. With the preponderance of Britain as a naval power, and the weakness of most European states, power politics were largely restricted to Britain, France and Russia. As between them competitive aggressiveness was recurrent: but, except briefly in the Pacific, and more frequently in the Near East and on the borders of India, their rivalry did not produce any major competition for new territory. And this seemed to imply that the end of mercantilism had been followed by the end also of political imperialism, which in turn suggested that the renewal of a general international desire for colonies after 1870 must have sprung from some new phenomenon—the unprecedented need to acquire openings for the safe investment of surplus capital.

It is mainly because Hobson's theory of "imperialism" in his own time was based on this theory of discontinuity in nineteenth-century history that it must be regarded as fallacious. For there had, in fact, been no break in the continuity of imperial development; merely a short-term variation in the methods used, corresponding with a temporary change in world conditions. In the first place, the extension of the territorial possessions of the three surviving great powers continued intermittently throughout: and the list of British acquisitions between 1840 and 1871 alone bears comparison with those of the following thirty years. On what grounds, in this period of so-called "anti-imperialism," are these to be explained? Obviously no single explanation will serve. Hong Kong stood alone as a trading base with a specifically economic function. Queensland was the result of internal expansion in Australia, [and] British Columbia of rivalry from the United States. But the rest—the Punjab, Sind, Berar, Oudh and Lower Burma on the frontiers of British India; Basutoland, Griqualand and (temporarily) the Transvaal on the Cape frontier; and small areas around existing trading bases in West Africa—stand as evidence that an existing empire will tend always to expand its boundaries. They were not the product of an expansive British policy, but of the need for military security, for administrative efficiency, or for the protection of indigenous peoples on the frontiers of existing colonies. Basically, they demonstrated the fact, familiar in earlier centuries, that colonies which exist in a power vacuum will tend always to expand slowly until they meet with some immovable political or geographical obstacle; and that a metropolitan government can do little more than slow down the speed of movement. For the purpose of the present argument this process may be said to indicate that Hobson needed no new explanation for the bulk of British acquisitions after 1870: for, as has already been pointed out, most of the new colonies on his list differed little in type or situation from those just mentioned—and were indeed mostly the extension of the same colonial frontiers. And, to this extent, late-nineteenth-century imperialism was merely the continuation of a process which had begun centuries earlier.

At the same time, it must be said that this "contiguous area" theory does not fully cover certain of the new British possessions on Hobson's list. For some of them, like East Africa, were not strictly contiguous to an existing British colony; and others, such as Nigeria or Rhodesia, were clearly annexed too suddenly and on too large a scale to be seen as the product of the domestic needs of Lagos or the Cape. These therefore suggest that some other factor was at work—competition for new colonies on political grounds —which will be considered later. . . .

It is now possible to place the imperialism of the period of Hobson's *Study* in its historical context, and to attempt a definition of the extent to which it differed from that of earlier years. The most obvious fact on which his theory was based was that, by contrast with the preceding half-century, vast areas of the world were quickly brought under European control for the first time: and it is now evident that this cannot be explained in terms of either of the two tendencies operating throughout the earlier nineteenth century. Although the break with the past was not as sharp as Hobson seemed to think, it remains true that many British annexations cannot be explained on the contiguous area theory; and the new possessions of France, Italy and Germany were quite definitely in a different category. But neither can these facts be explained on Hobson's theory for, as has been said, the places now to be taken over had hitherto attracted little capital, and did not attract it in any quantity subsequently. Nor, again, can an explanation be found in the more general theory of economic imperialism, for these places in the Pacific and in Africa for which the nations now competed were of marginal economic importance; and, on the assumptions of the past fifty years, governments might have been expected to reject demands by their nationals for annexation of territories whose administrative costs would be out of all proportion to their economic value to the nation. In sum, the most obvious facts of the new phase of imperialism cannot be explained as the logical continuation of the recent past, nor in Hobson's terms of a new economic factor. What, then, was the explanation?

An answer is not, of course, hard to find, and indeed emerges clearly from the vast literature now available. With the exception of the supporters of the "imperialism" thesis, the consensus of opinion is very marked. The new factor in imperialism was not something without precedent, certainly not anything uniquely economic, but essentially a throwback to some of the characteristic attitudes and practices of the eighteenth century. Just as, in the early nineteenth century, the economic interests had demanded effectively that imperial questions should no longer be decided on political grounds, demanding opulence in place of security, so, at the end of the century, the balance was again reversed. The outstanding feature of the new situation was the subordination of economic to political considerations, the preoccupation with national security, military power and prestige.

Again, reasons are not hard to find. The significant fact about the years after 1870 was that Europe became once again an armed camp. The creation of a united Germany, the defeat of Austria and, above all, of France were to dominate European thinking until 1914. Between Germany and France there stood the question of Alsace-Lorraine: and for both the primary consideration was now a system of alliances which would, on the German side, prevent French counterattack [and], on the French side, make revenge possible. Inevitably the rest of Europe was drawn into the politics of the balance of power between them; and for all statesmen military strength became once again the criterion of national greatness. Inevitably too this situation, with its similarities to the politics of the eighteenth century, brought in its train a return to many of the attitudes of mercantilism. Emigration to foreign states, instead of being regarded as an economic safety valve, became once again a loss of military or manufacturing manpower; and population statistics became a measure of relative national strength. Protective tariffs came back also, with the primary aim of building up national self-sufficiency and the power to make war.

Under such circumstances it was only to be expected that colonies would be regarded once again as assets in the struggle for power and status: but in fact the attitude of the powers to the imperial question was not at first a simple one. Indeed, it cannot be said that the attitudes characteristic of the imperialism of free trade were seriously weakened until the mid-1880s; and until then it seemed possible that the colonial question might be kept clear of European politics. This is not in fact surprising. For most of the men who then ruled Europe retained a realistic appreciation of the potential value to their countries of those parts of the world that were available for annexation. . . .

In a narrow sense, then, the race for colonies was the product of diplomacy rather than of any more positive force. Germany set the example by claiming exclusive control over areas in which she had an arguable commercial stake, but no more, as a means of adding a new dimension to her international bargaining power, both in respect of what she had already taken, and of what she might claim in the future. Thereafter the process could not be checked; for, under conditions of political tension, the fear of being left out of the partition of the globe overrode all practical considerations. Perhaps Britain was the only country which showed genuine reluctance to take a share; and this was due both to her immense stake in the continuance of the status quo for reasons of trade, and to her continued realism in assessing the substantive value of the lands under dispute. And the fact that she too joined in the competition demonstrated how contagious the new political forces were. Indeed, until the end of the century, imperialism may best be seen as the extension into the periphery of the political struggle in Europe. At the center the balance was so nicely adjusted that no positive action, no major change in the status or territory of either side was possible. Colonies thus became a means out of the impasse. . . .

This analysis of the dynamic force of the new imperialism has been stated in purely political terms. What part was played in it by the many nonpolitical interests with a stake in the new colonies: the traders, the investors, the missionaries, and the speculators? For these were the most vociferous exponents of a forward policy in most countries: and to men like Hobson it seemed that their influence, if backed by that of the greater interest of the financier, was decisive in causing the politicians to act.

Again the problem is complex. In general terms the answer would seem to be that, while statesmen were very much aware of the pressure groups—conscious of the domestic political advantage of satisfying their demands, and often themselves sympathetic to the case they put up—they were not now, any more than earlier in the century, ready to undertake the burden of new colonies simply on their account. What made it seem as if these interests were now calling the tune was that the choice facing the statesmen was no longer between annexation and the continued independence of the area in question: it was now between action and allowing a rival to step in. Salisbury and Rosebery may well have been convinced by the argument of men like Lugard that, on humanitarian grounds, it would be desirable for Britain to bring law and order to Uganda. But it was the threat of German or French occupation of the key to the Nile and Egypt that decided them to act. Yet if, in the last resort, the decision by Britain or any other country to annex was based on the highest reasons of state, it is also true that the very existence of these hitherto embarrassing pressure groups now became a diplomatic asset, since they were the obvious grounds on which valid claims could be made, an approximation to the principle of effective occupation.

Thus the relative importance of the concrete interests and demands of the various pressure groups, as compared with the political criteria of the statesmen, was the reverse of that assigned to them by Hobson; and, if the word "investment" is taken to cover the whole range of these interests, the point has been well summarized by Professor E. Staley:

Conflicts between the great powers over private investment matters have rarely, almost never, reached a state of dangerous international tension except in cases where the powers have been led into conflict by the pursuit of political policies extraneous to the investment affair itself. The best explanation of these facts runs in terms of the way in which those in charge of foreign policies interpret national advantage. Where investments can be regarded as economic aids to established lines of foreign policy, they are supported most vigorously; investments receive least vigorous political backing where they are not in any sense tools of national policy or where they run counter to national policy.

By the end of the century, the "imperial idea," as it has significantly been called, after twenty years of propaganda by such groups of enthusiasts as the German *Kolonialverein* and the British Imperial Federation League, had become dominant. The process of educating the public has now been examined in detail, and it is interesting to see that in each case the historian has found it necessary to deal almost entirely in ideas rather than in concrete facts. This is no accident. The imperialism of the early twentieth century, although ironically the product of the power politics of the previous two decades, bore little resemblance to the ideas of men like Bismarck and Salisbury. It was the generation of Kaiser Wilhelm II, of Theodore Roosevelt and of Chamberlain (in his later years) that came to adopt for the first time this mystical faith in the value of an empire. Chamberlain's tariff campaign of 1903-1905 indicates that such tenuous links as the imperial movement had ever had with precise calculations of economic—and even of political—advantage had now ceased to be of primary importance.

For by that time, imperialism had been shown to be a delusion. It was already the common experience of all the countries that had taken part in the partition of Africa and the Pacific that, except for the few windfalls, such as gold in West Africa, diamonds in South West Africa, and copper in the Congo and Rhodesia, the new colonies were white elephants: and that only small sectional interests in any country had obtained real benefits from them. Whether German,

French, British or Italian, their trade was minute (German trade with her colonies was only 1/2 percent of her external trade); their attraction for investors, except in mines, etc., was negligible; they were unsuitable for large-scale emigration, and any economic development that had taken place was usually the result of determined efforts by the European state concerned to create an artificial asset. Moreover, in most cases, the cost of administration was a deadweight on the imperial power. By 1900 all these facts were apparent and undeniable. They were constantly pressed by opponents of colonial expansion in each country; and Hobson's book consisted primarily of an exposition of these defects. Yet public opinion was increasingly oblivious to such facts: the possession of colonies had become a sacred cow, a psychological necessity. While the financiers continued to invest their money as they had done in the previous fifty years, in economically sound projects such as the Baghdad railway, in the nontropical settlement colonies and independent countries, and in places like India—remaining true to the criteria of true economic imperialism—the politicians, pressed on now by a public demand they could not control, even if they had wanted to, continued, with increasing bellicosity, to scrape the bottom of the barrel for yet more colonial burdens for the white man to carry.

The reassessment of so abstract a concept as "imperialism," particularly within the present limitations of space, cannot hope to prove or to disprove anything. At the most it may lead to the suggestion that an earlier synthesis does not appear to fit the facts. How far can it be said that the arguments put forward above make necessary a revision of the theory of imperialism which derives from Hobson and Lenin?

The general conclusion would seem to emerge that, as a historical interpretation of the expansion of European empires between 1870 and 1914, it is unacceptable. As an economic theory it is unsatisfactory because detailed investigations have shown that the alleged need of the European investor, monopolist or individual capitalist to find outlets for his surplus capital had little or nothing to do with the division of Africa and the Pacific between the European powers. Again, as a theory of historical development, which makes this expansion seem to be a unique phenomenon, capable of being understood only in terms of the special methodology used by Hobson and Lenin, it ignores both the continuity of nineteenth-century developments, and also its similarity to earlier periods of Eurpoean imperialism. In most respects, indeed, there was no break in continuity after 1870. On the political side, many of the new annexations of territory, particularly those made by Britain, resulted from the situation of existing possessions: and, on the economic side, the rapid expansion of European commercial and financial influence throughout the world—the true "economic imperialism"—did not change its character after 1870; and was no more likely then than before to have resulted in significant acquisitions of land. The real break in the continuity of nineteenth-century development—the rapid extension of "formal" control over independent areas of Africa and the East—was a specifically political phenomenon in origin, the outcome of fears and rivalries within Europe. The competition for colonies, being as characteristic of economically weak countries like Italy as of others which had large resources of capital available for overseas deployment, was indeed more obviously a throwback to the imperialism of the eighteenth century than the characteristic product of nineteenth-century capitalism in an advanced phase. And the ideological fervor that became the dominant feature of the imperial movement after about 1890 was the natural outcome of this fevered nationalism, not the artifact of vested economic interests. . . .

In the second half of the twentieth century, it can be seen that imperialism owed its popular appeal not to the sinister influence of the capitalists, but to its inherent attractions for the masses. In the new quasi-democratic Europe, the popularity of the imperial idea marked a rejection of the sane morality of the account-book, and the adoption of a creed based on such irrational concepts as racial superiority and the prestige of the nation. Whether we interpret it, as did J. A. Schumpeter in 1919, as a castback to the ideas of the old autocratic monarchies of the *ancien régime,* or as something altogether new—the first of the irrational myths that have dominated the first half of the twentieth century—it is clear that imperialism cannot be explained in simple terms of economic theory and the nature of finance capitalism. In its mature form it can best be described as a sociological phenomenon with roots in political facts: and it can properly be understood only in terms of the same social hysteria that has since given birth to other and more disastrous forms of aggressive nationalism.

Henri Brunschwig

COLONIES, AN UNPROFITABLE VENTURE

Henri Brunschwig (1904-   ), the leading French historian of French overseas expansion, has published, among other works, *French Colonialism 1871-1914, Myths and Realities* (1966). He retired in 1977 from the prestigious Ecole Pratique des Hautes Etudes.

In this selection, taken from *French Colonialism,* Brunschwig shows the negative balance sheet of French imperialism. He finds that the French empire was not a paying proposition: while it paid in pride and glory, it cost in francs.

IN 1890, Jules Ferry published a small book entitled *Le Tonkin et la mère patrie.* Its first section of fifty-five pages was subtitled "Five Years Afterwards." The rest of the book consisted of "eyewitness accounts" of Tongking collected by Léon Sentupéry, who has often incorrectly been described as the book's author. In the first chapter, Ferry seeks at the outset to correct prevalent "misconceptions" about the expenses incurred in the conquest of Tongking. He then advances certain views on the unpopularity which colonial policy encountered in the France of his day, and recalls that it had been no less unpopular in the past. . . .

The economic aspect—which Ferry always regarded as essential—is to him a matter of finding outlets, for when he speaks of "investment colonies" (*colonies de capitaux*), he appears to be thinking only of trade. The chief novelty in the book, compared with the speech, is his long description of the "protectionist system" which in his argument becomes the essential cause of expansion. Since his day, many historians and economists have traced the same sequence of events: industrialization as the cause of protectionism, which in its turn leads to overproduction, the outcome of which is the need for colonial markets. This appears so logical that it is very easy to be persuaded by the well-known attraction of proof by three-stage syllogism. However, closer investigation does not bear out this theory. . . .

Ferry had set France upon an imperialist course with the Tunis Expedition of 1881, but it was not until 1892 that the French parliament endorsed protection by voting for the Méline tariff. At this time the McKinley tariff, voted in 1890, had already made the United States protectionist, but the Americans waited a further eight years before engaging in imperialism in the shape of its seizure of the Spanish colonies of Cuba, Puerto Rico and the Philippines (1898). Yet it was not economic circles which advocated these ventures. What is more: the fact that Britain, Belgium and the

Reprinted with permission from Henri Brunschwig, *French Colonialism 1871-1914, Myths and Realities,* translated by William Glanville Brown (London: Pall Mall Press, 1964), pp. 82, 85-87, 89-90, 94-96, 135-136, 138-139, 151.

Netherlands remained free-trade countries did not prevent their acquiring colonies. This simple confrontation of dates should make us suspicious of the theory that protectionism leads to colonial expansion.

Jules Ferry explained that exclusion from the markets of countries which became protectionist compelled nations which were not protectionist to seek outlets elsewhere. But on what did he base his argument? It was easy to verify the facts. Germany's protective tariff came into force in 1879; France remained a free-trade country until 1892. . . .France's total trade with Germany increased from 882.8 million francs in 1878 to 883.9 in 1879, to 945.5 in 1880, to 981 in 1881, and to 993.2 in 1882. If we examine the relationship between imports and exports, we notice that France until the end of the century continued to import more than it exported. The two graphs remain parallel until 1885, after which France gradually redressed the balance, and between 1892 and 1908, exported more than it imported. . . .

It has to be noted that there is nothing whatever in the figures to support the theory that colonial outlets diminished the trade gap. The Tunisian expedition took place in 1881, when the figures of general trade were the highest since 1870. The conquest of Madagascar in 1895 and the occasions when France intervened in Morocco after 1905, all occurred at times when trade was booming. The only conquest occurring at a time when trade was diminishing was that of Tongking, between 1883 and 1885.

The general picture which emerges is that the results of colonial expansion do not show on the graph of external trade. . . .

Colonial expansion was unquestionably followed by an increase in trade between France and its colonies. . . .The *General Table of France's External Trade* gives us, averaged over a five-year period, the percentage of France's total external trade both with foreign countries and also with its colonies and protectorates. The following figures are taken from this table:

	Foreign Countries		Colonies & Protectorates	
	Imports	Exports	Imports	Exports
	%	%	%	%
1882-1886	95.30	93.27	4.70	6.73
1886-1890	93.89	93.46	6.11	6.54
1891-1895	92.45	91.56	7.55	8.44
1896-1900	92.19	90.16	7.81	9.84
1901-1905	91.43	89.38	8.57	10.62
1906-1910	90.85	89.51	9.15	10.49
1909-1913	90.72	89.08	9.28	10.92

So, if one takes imports and exports together, between 1882-1886 and 1909-1913 the percentage went up from 5.71 percent to 10.2 percent, which is a negligible amount if one remembers that in France foreign trade was only a small proportion of total trade, internal and external. . . .

Confining myself to the period after 1900 and the completion of the conquest, and regrouping the figures published by the Office Colonial, I have drawn up the following table, which excludes Algeria and Tunisia, these being the territories showing the largest debit balance.

IMPORTS (in francs)

Year	From France	From the French Colonies	From Foreign Countries
1901	245,198,544	20,437,169	208,975,169
1904	194,188,623	13,460,036	203,989,180
1905	225,826,358	12,495,436	250,757,697
1906	201,386,226	14,465,749	239,093,294
1907	219,943,727	16,618,340	292,845,262
1909	230,397,844	15,466,674	267,291,729
1910	238,687,839	— —	321,197,472

EXPORTS (in francs)

Year	To France	To the French Colonies	To Foreign Countries
1901	171,747,226	13,715,416	179,055,840
1904	157,587,448	8,406,259	209,190,506
1905	152,421,921	7,123,624	225,311,919
1906	179,276,468	8,568,573	232,483,267
1907	195,317,402	9,014,918	307,778,233
1909	247,562,616	9,876,294	317,955,192
1910	287,389,025	— —	377,178,139

It will be seen that, on the whole, the trade of <u>foreign countries benefited more than French trade from France's colonial expansion.</u>

FOREIGN TRADE WITH FRENCH COLONIES

Year	Total Trade[1]	Imports to Colonies[2]	Exports from Colonies[3]
	%	%	%
1894	46.0	49.0	56.0
1903	49.0	51.0	47.0
1904	52.5	49.0	56.0
1905	55.2	51.1	60.3
1906	46.1	47.5	44.7
1907	60.1	41.5	38.2
1908	56.6	55.2	58.0
1909	53.6	52.0	55.2
1910	56.9	57.3	56.7

[*Editor's note:*
[1] Percentage of total trade benefiting foreigners
[2] Percentage of total imports coming from foreign countries
[3] Percentage of total exports going to foreign countries]

It would be impossible to make this brief survey the basis for drawing conclusions about the economic value of colonies under the Third Republic. This would necessitate a far more thorough inquiry, including replacing the unreliable customs statistics by data obtained from chambers of commerce and from undertakings which made use of or dealt in colonial products, or operated mainly in overseas markets; and no doubt these would be difficult to obtain. Nevertheless, it is possible to draw a few general conclusions from this investigation.

1. The connection which Jules Ferry made between protectionism and colonization did not really exist. Expansion developed between 1880 and 1892 under a system of free trade, and continued after the introduction of protection under the Méline tariff of 1892. From 1900 onward, the leaders of the colonial party waxed indignant against this protectionist system.

2. The colonies did not supply French industry with a profitable monopoly. They could not have done so because French industry was not in a position to supply them. They were therefore obliged to obtain supplies from foreign countries, despite the customs duties which made these more expensive.

3. The policy of expansion certainly cost France more than it brought in. Does this mean that those who advocated it should have desisted? Not necessarily, for they could always hope for future benefits. This colonial policy essentially consisted of banking on the future. Credits are voted for the armed forces because of the dividends which will accrue after the conquest; investments are made because railways and other technical installations will enable the country to be properly exploited, and hospitals and schools are built in order to create a profitable labour force on the spot. There is constant speculation on the future and, in the last analysis, this speculation leads the colonizers to equip the colonial dependencies instead of purely and simply to exploit them. . . .

Colonial expansion was costly. The members of the Chamber, whom governments called upon to vote credits, very soon asked themselves whether the game was worth the candle. The Colonial Ministry's Estimates kept going up. In 1885 they stood at 42,652,000 francs, in 1894 at 79,018,500 francs and in 1900 at 89,768,262 francs, but at the end of that financial year actual expenditure was found to have amounted to 106,000,500 francs. The largest Estimates were in 1902, when expenditure amounted to 115,960,545 francs. The Finance Law of 1900 gave the overseas possessions budgetary autonomy and, by giving effect to this, it subsequently became possible to reduce France's subsidies to local colonial budgets. The Ministry's Estimates then came down to 98,269,689 francs in 1907, but went up to 104,964,905 francs in 1913.

The importance of these figures is only relative, for they do not represent the cost of the policy of colonial expansion. This is, first, because they do not cover the territories of North Africa, which were administered by other ministries. Furthermore, other ministries (Justice, Public Education, War and Navy) helped to meet colonial expenditure. Lastly, certain expenses would have to be deducted from them, in particular those having to do with the administration of penitentiaries, which usually came to between eight and nine million francs.

Over four fifths of these Estimates almost always went on the armed forces. . . . This expenditure on the armed forces covered transport, the stationing of troops, their rations and supplies, hospitals, and the colonies' defense preparedness. The Estimates also covered administering and policing the colonies, but their capital equipment was mainly covered by loans. . . .

Responsible politicians inevitably asked themselves, questions of doctrine apart, whether what was taking place was profitable. The first man who frankly asked the question was Turrel, the Chamber's rapporteur for the Colonial Estimates of 1896, and deputy for Aude. . . .

In his capacity as rapporteur for the Colonial Estimates of 1896, Turrel circulated a supplementary report dealing with the figures of 1894, and raising the question as to whether the policy of colonial expansion was a paying proposition. The report said: . . .

1. Our colonies do more trade with foreign countries than with France. 2. The colonies import, i.e. purchase, from abroad more than they do from France: colonial imports from France are 28 million francs less in value than colonial imports from foreign countries. 3. The colonies have a favourable balance of trade with foreign countries of only 10 million francs, but their favourable balance with France amounts to 23 million—and this despite the fact that our colonies do 46 million francs' less trade with France than they do with foreign countries.

These facts indisputably prove that the colonial market is dominated by foreigners. When considering and evaluating these figures of exports to the colonies, it must not be forgotten that our trade with them differs essentially from that of foreigners who, when they sell goods, withdraw the whole amount paid for them. It can in fact be said that the 124 million francs' worth of foreign imports into our colonies represents a transfer of 124 million francs from our colonies to foreign countries. Moreover, the 95 million francs' worth of French exports to our colonies is mostly for our army and our officials and is therefore paid for out of the French budget. When the Colonial Ministry appoints a colonial official and he buys something from France, he pays for it out of his salary, which comes out of the French budget. This can scarcely be thought a profitable arrangement for France since, in order to export goods worth 95 million francs, we first spend 80 million francs annually, money which is a charge on the French budget.

The position may be summarized thus: Outlets worth 95 million francs cost us 80 million francs a year; foreign countries have outlets in our colonies worth 126 million, for which they make no preliminary expenditure. If the analysis be carried further, it will be found that our trade with the colonies gives them a profit of 23 million francs. Our trade relationship with them could, therefore, be summed up thus: On the trade France does with its colonies as a whole, France loses 23 million francs a year: to achieve which result the country spends 80 million francs. . . .

In France there was no income tax, so we lack the kind of statistics which Hobson was able to make use of in order to reveal exactly what profits individuals made out of the colonies and who benefited from them. Was it they whose pressure caused governments to carry out a policy of expansion which was not profitable for the nation as a whole? Was it because the French were counting on future profits? Or was it a feeling of nationalism which made it impossible for them to withdraw from a general competition, every success in which gave a feeling of pride to the citizens of the nation which had triumphed?

It is difficult to tell how important each factor was, but it cannot be denied that, if nationalism had not coloured the whole of this period, it would in the long run have been impossible for a small group of profiteers to insist on the carrying out of a policy which enormously increased the budget. This is why, as we shall see, the "colonialists" seized every opportunity to repeat the arguments of geographical societies and to beat the patriotic drum.

Hans-Ulrich Wehler

SOCIAL AND ECONOMIC CRISES

Hans-Ulrich Wehler (1931-   ), professor of history at the University of Bielefeld, Germany, has published several works dealing with the social and political history of nineteenth-century Germany, the best known being *Bismarck und der Imperialismus* (1969). In this selection he argues that the desire of the German government to heal the rift between labor and capital, to provide an outlet for new trade, thus to avoid further depressions and an exacerbation of class conflict, led Bismarck to take up an imperialist course. Imperialism, motivated by social considerations at home, is known as "social imperialism." Wehler provides one of the most sophisticated interpretations of this phenomenon.

G ERMAN imperialism during the Bismarckian era remains a controversial topic. There is disagreement about both its underlying causes and development, and its historical significance. Numerous problems still remain a *terra incognita* for the historian. Above all the question of the continuity of German imperialism from the time of expansion through free trade in the 1850s and 1860s up until Hitler's *Ostland* imperialism still requires close investigation; only the main lines of development can as yet be clearly discerned.

The present state of the debate is in part due to the fact that until a few years ago the most important historical sources—state papers and manuscript collections—were still inaccessible to scholars. Since this is no longer the case, it is possible to make a fresh attempt to analyze these problems, proceeding from surer foundations. This, however, is only one prerequisite, albeit an important one. Very much more to blame for the

present state of research into German imperialism has been the lack of an adequate theory.

This is the reason why important interrelationships and possible explanations have so far been overlooked. The historiography of imperialism urgently needs a critical historical theory before it can provide illuminating analyses and explanations of socioeconomic and political processes. I have tried elsewhere to develop in detail such a critical historical theory of imperialism, based on that nineteenth-century phenomenon which was most decisive for world history—namely industrialization, and its attendant social and political developments. Such a theory, like any theory in the social sciences, has to satisfy certain requirements: first, it has to combine a maximum of empirically obtained and verifiable information with as much explanatory power as possible; second, it should cover a variety of similar phenomena—it must in this case

Reprinted from Hans-Ulrich Wehler, "Bismarck's Imperialism, 1862-1890," *Past and Present*, No. 48 (1970), pp. 119-127, 131-137, 139-144, 146-149. World Copyright: The Past and Present Society, Corpus Christi College, Oxford, England. The extracts from this article are reprinted with the permission of the Society and the author from *Past and Present: A Journal of Historical Studies*, No. 48 (August 1970).

enable the historian to compare the modern western forms of imperialism. From this theory of imperialism—which aims to establish a link between the problems of economic growth in industrialized countries and the changes in their social and political structure—two elements call for discussion here, which are particularly important for the explanatory model.

1. One of the dangerous legends of contemporary development-politics is the belief that rapid economic growth promotes social and political stability, and inhibits radical and irresponsible policies. Historical experience has shown, however, that rapid growth produces extremely acute economic, social and political problems. Germany is a particularly illuminating case. Here, after the breakthrough of the industrial revolution 1834/50-1873, industrialization was necessarily associated with a large number of profound difficulties in Germany's internal development. More than half a century ago, Thorstein Veblen stated the basic problem: the absorption of the most advanced technology by a largely traditional society within a then unprecedentedly short time. And one of the most important contemporary experts on the problems of economic growth, Alexander Gerschenkron, had the German experience particularly in mind, when he propounded his general theory that the faster and the more abrupt a country's industrial revolution, the more intractable and complex will be the problems associated with industrialization. After the period from the onset of the German Industrial Revolution until the second world economic crisis of 1873, there followed a period of intensive industrialization, punctuated by lengthy interruptions in the process of economic growth (the three industrial depressions of 1873-79, 1882-86 and 1890-95, together with the structural crisis of agriculture from 1876 onwards), and accompanied by social upheavals in which many contemporaries saw the approach of social revolution. In other words, the problems of uneven economic growth, together with all its effects, were of immense importance in Bismarck's Germany. It was also as a reaction against

this partly rapid, partly disturbed, in any case uneven growth that the system of organized capitalism of the large-scale enterprises developed as a means of bringing about stability and the social control of industrial development. Organized capitalism grew up in the period before 1896 (that "watershed between two epochs in the social history of capitalism," as the young Schumpeter called it), so that one can see the period from 1873 to 1896 as an extremely difficult structural crisis in the development of the modern industrial system. The same period saw the beginnings of the modern interventionist state, which similarly sought to master the problems of uneven industrial growth. Both the interventionist state and organized capitalism saw a pragmatic, anticyclical economic policy as an important means of stabilization. Therefore, both attached decisive importance to the promotion of an export offensive and to the winning of foreign markets—either through the methods of informal empire or through direct colonial rule. This was considered of decisive importance both for economic prosperity and for domestic social stability—for the same reasons a sort of law of the increasing importance of foreign trade during times of economic depression and crisis still seems to be valid today. The welfare of the country was therefore made dependent on the successes of informal and formal expansion. Since the preservation of the traditional social hierarchy was often the dominant motive behind expansion, one is justified in talking of a social imperialism. In Germany, there began to develop a broad ideological consensus of agreement to this effect from the end of the first depression (1878-1879) onwards, and subsequent German overseas expansionism rested upon this consensus.

2. Bismarck's greater Prussian Imperial State as founded in 1871, was the product of the "revolution from above" in its military stage. The legitimacy of the young Reich had no generally accepted basis nor was it founded upon a generally accepted code of basic political convictions, as was to be immediately demonstrated in the years of

crisis after 1873. Bismarck had to cover up the social and political differences in the tension-ridden class society of his new Germany, and to this end he relied on a technique of negative integration. His method was to inflame the conflicts between those groups which were allegedly hostile to the Reich, the *Reichsfeinde,* like the Socialists and Catholics, left-wing Liberals and Jews on the one hand, and those groups which were allegedly loyal to the Reich, the *Reichsfreunde.* It was thanks to the permanent conflict between these in- and outgroups that he was able to achieve variously composed majorities for his policies. The Chancellor was thus under constant pressure to provide rallying points for his *Reichspolitik,* and to legitimize his system by periodically producing fresh political successes. Within a typology of contemporary power structures in the second half of the nineteenth century Bismarck's régime can be classified as a Bonapartist dictatorship: a traditional, unstable social and political structure which found itself threatened by strong forces of social and political change, was to be defended and stabilized by diverting attention away from constitutional policy towards economic policy, away from the question of emancipation at home towards compensatory successes abroad; these ends were to be further achieved by undisguised repression as well as by limited concessions. In this way also the neo-absolutist, pseudo-constitutional dictatorship of the Chancellor could be maintained. By guaranteeing the bourgeoisie protection from the workers' demands for political and social emancipation in exchange for its own political abdication, the dictatorial executive gained a noteworthy degree of political independence vis-à-vis the component social groups and economic interests. And just as overseas expansion, motivated by domestic and economic consideration, had become an element of the political style of French Bonapartism, so Bismarck too, after a short period of consolidation in foreign affairs, saw the advantages of such expansion as an antidote to recurring economic setbacks and to the permanent direct or latent threat to

the whole system and became the "Caesarist statesman."

Early German imperialism can also be viewed as the initial phase of an apparently contemporary phenomenon. Jürgen Habermas has demonstrated recently how, under the present system of state-regulated capitalism, political power is legitimized chiefly by a deliberate policy of state intervention which tries to correct the disfunctions of the economy—in particular disturbances of economic growth—in order to ensure the stability of the economic system. The demand for "legitimation" to which these societies are subject, leads to a situation in which a "substitute programme" replaces the discredited ideology of the liberal-capitalist market economy. Ruling elites are thereby obliged to do two things if they wish to preserve the system and their own vested interests. First, they must ensure that favourable "conditions for stability be maintained for the entire social system and that risks for economic growth be avoided." Second, they must "pursue a policy of avoiding conflict by granting compensations in order to ensure the loyalty of the wage-earning masses." Thus, planned "scientific and technological progress," the main productive force of our times, and a steady rate of economic growth, assume increasingly the function of legitimizing political power. These problems do not have an exclusively modern significance. Their historical genesis can be traced back to the last third of the nineteenth century. In Germany, as has already been stated, their origins can be clearly traced back to the Bismarckian era. It may be illuminating to view German imperialism during these years—like many other actions of the developing interventionist state—as an attempt on the part of her ruling elites to create improved conditions favourable to the stability of the social and economic systems as it stood. They had realized that the traditional and charismatic authority of the government was losing its effectiveness.

In creating better conditions for social and economic stability, they thus hoped to take the heat out of internal disputes about the distribution of the national income and of political power, and at the same time provide new foundations for the rule of an authoritarian leadership and of privileged social groups. Bismarck's Bonapartist and dictatorial régime together with the social forces which supported it, and later on particularly the exponents of *Weltpolitik*, expected that economic and social imperialism would legitimate their authority. Critical observers at the time also recognized this fact quite clearly.

From a consideration of these two theoretical questions—first, the problems of uneven economic growth, and second, the need for an authoritarian system to legitimate itself—there emerges one fundamental point for the following discussion: German imperialism is to be seen primarily as the result of *endogenous* socioeconomic and political forces, and not as a reaction to *exogenous* pressure, nor as a means of defending traditional foreign interests. . . .

In view of the long controversy over Bismarck's motives for "entering the arena of *Weltpolitik*," one decisive point must first of all be made and emphasized: in Bismarck's overseas policies there is a remarkable continuity of both the ideas and the methods of free-trade commercial expansionism; he adhered to this particular policy of expansion from 1862 until 1898 because he clearly recognized the financial burdens, the political responsibilities as well as the military risks that were involved in formal colonial rule. He was influenced too by the enormous success of Britain's mid-Victorian Informal Empire, and at the same time he carefully calculated the importance of those interests which could be satisfied by a laissez-faire overseas policy. The years 1884-1886 did not see a sudden revision of his basic ideas, nor did they see a sudden change of mind, a sudden enthusiasm for colonies. There were, however, some motives which, contrary to his previous experience and hopes, induced Bismarck for some time to involve the state in the governance of Protectorates. It is indisputable that he would have preferred to hand these territories over to syndicates of private interest-groups as trading colonies, with some form of loosely formalized imperial protection. Thereafter too, Bismarck remained convinced that Informal Empire was preferable to colonies under formal state administration. He persisted, moreover, in the belief that economic interests should take the initiative overseas and that the state should merely follow later, without seeing its goal from the very beginning as formal colonial rule. As the colonial publicist, Friedrich Fabri, noted with regret as late as 1889, the "colonial-political programme of the Reich government" was "based on the principle of *laissez-aller.*"

It seems hardly possible to dispute this continuity in Bismarck's basic ideas. Only if great prestige value were attached to colonies as the necessary attributes of a world power, or if—contrary to much historical evidence—colonies were considered to be economically more valuable than Informal Empire, could this continuity be denied or overlooked. It is not this continuity of intention which poses the real problems, but rather its relationship to the heterogeneous methods employed in the Protectorate policy of the 1880s.

If, however, one is convinced by the consistency of Bismarck's statements regarding his basic imperial conception over three decades—the laissez-faire expansion offered the most advantages—then his policy up to 1884 appears quite logical, and shows that he was not just waiting for a favourable opportunity to acquire colonies. Above all, the apparent contradiction between the establishment of Protectorates and his repeated criticism of colonies is then largely resolved. In 1884-1886 Bismarck would unquestionably have preferred to avoid the formal acquisition of colonies—on economic and commercial grounds; and for Bismarck, the acquisition of colonies remained a means, rather than an end in itself. The irony of his colonial policy, against which the free-trade Liberals protested so sharply, consists precisely in the fact that he shared for most of the time the misgivings of these critics. He was, therefore, quite sincere when he assured the French Ambassador De Courcel as late as the autumn of 1884, that "the aim of German policy" was only the expansion of unrestricted trade, and not "the territorial expansion of German colonial possessions. . . ."

Why did Bismarck decide in the mid-1880s that it was no longer possible merely to opt for free-trade expansion? Why—hesitantly and with many reservations—did he come round to the view that it was necessary to assume formal colonial rule? He saw his own policies as a response to the exigencies of the socioeconomic and political system. In Germany, as elsewhere, the new period of depression beginning in 1882 had a catalytic effect on imperialist policies. This change clearly had its antecedents: since 1879 support of the overseas trade offensive had been considered one of the tasks of the interventionist state. But it was not until the shock effects of the second depression were felt after 1882, that state assistance in this sphere was intensified. After the autumn of 1882, when there was the threat of a repetition of the grim experiences of 1873-1879 and of a further interruption in economic growth, the traumatic effects of the first depression were deepened. The safeguarding of the home market through protectionist measures, which had for some time been considered the most effective anticyclical device, proved to be of little use when the worldwide slump began. A crisis in agriculture coincided with the depression in industry; the agrarian and industrial elites were hard-hit. Social tensions became more acute; the "red peril" developed in industrial areas; a feeling that the country was in a state of crisis became more and more widespread; Bismarck's Bonapartist régime and his policy of the "conservative alliance" were faced with a severe test. Confronted with the effects that uneven industrial growth was producing in the economic, social and political spheres, the political leaders in Berlin could not stand idly by—extensive expansion overseas was one of the countermeasures which aimed at easing this critical situation. "Industrial development which has resulted in overproduction drives Germany to seek the acquisition of colonies"—the opinion of France's representative in Berlin was shared by numerous other observers. . . .

The policy which led to the acquisition of colonies in Africa and in the Pacific was only one of the methods whereby the state promoted foreign trade. There is little doubt that the "open door policy" remained Bismarck's ideal—he was still able to pursue it in China and in the Congo. If England and France had guaranteed free trade in Africa, unrestricted commercial expansion of this sort would have entirely satisfied Bismarck's economic aims—it was his view that, under these circumstances, German interests engaged in overseas competition could have asserted and extended themselves with limited governmental support. But the crucial reasons which induced him from 1883-1884 onwards to seek a gradual formalization of imperial control in Africa and the Pacific were twofold: on the one hand internal pressure resulting from the crisis was mounting and had to be reduced; on the other, the end of the free-trade era appeared imminent, and increasing competition together with the use of protectionist methods by other powers made direct state involvement overseas inevitable. In other words, the obvious disadvantages of the state continuing to play a passive role were beginning to outweigh the equally obvious disadvantages of increased state activity. In West Africa a complete dependence of Germany on other colonial powers with protective, differential, and even prohibitive tariffs seemed imminent. In South Africa, East Africa and New Guinea, Great Britain and Australia seemed to be on the verge of seizing further territory. It was believed in Berlin that unless the government acted, these rivals with their "preclusive imperialism" would gain ascendancy. There was an unmistakable fear of being left out in the cold, of arriving too late for the progressive sharing-out of the territorial spoils of the non-occidental world. The press constantly repeated that Germany should not stand idly by while "other nations appropriate great tracts of territory and the very rich natural resources that go with them," waiting until "nothing is left for us from this economic conquest of the as yet unexploited parts of the earth." The government assured the *Reichstag* that "the expansionist colonial policies of other powers" compelled Germany to similar action "unless she wished to be totally excluded from the partition of the world." The imperialism of the 1880s derived not so much from irrepressible feelings of strength and vitality, as has often been claimed, but rather from the incapacity of the industrial states to deal with the internal problems caused by an explosive and unstable industrialization. Just as at home leading landowners and industrialists were driven together to form a "cartel of fear" in the face of economic crises and social revolution, and to pursue an expansionist policy as a way out of these difficulties, so were the rival industrial states united in their overseas policies by their suspicions that they might miss out on something decisive if they held back. . . .

This feeling of being excluded from the exploitation of undeveloped countries was constantly nurtured by pressure groups with vested interests. Woermann, Lüderitz and Peters repeatedly pointed to the strong foreign competition to which they might succumb. Because it was then difficult to obtain reliable information about what was happening overseas, the state often acted on the narrow basis of reports from pressure groups. Even an official of the Foreign Office who favoured colonial expansion considered in 1885 that "too much importance is attached to the wishes and claims of interested private individuals." But when he criticized a Hamburg merchant, active in trade with Africa, for presenting his personal interests as though they were identical with "the interests of the fatherland," Bismarck at once reproached him: "All business affairs are by their very nature selfish," but what is to the advantage of the Hamburg merchant "is also to the advantage of the country as a whole and forms a small part of our national interest." Bismarck gradually yielded to the pincer movement from without and within, to the threatening dangers of overseas competition and to the warnings of the interest groups that he should not let chances go

begging during the time of the depression. His prophylactic expansionism sought to protect present advantages and potential opportunities from the claims of rival powers in such a way that he eventually had to pay the price of formal colonial rule. In these respects his methods and the motives behind them were unquestionably similar to those of the "preclusive imperialism" then being pursued in London, particularly vis-à-vis Germany. It cannot be demonstrated that Bismarck would have assumed formal protectorates in overseas areas without the real or latent threat that rival states would beat him to it. . . .

Above all, overseas expansion remained for Bismarck a question of economic policy, and here too, he did not adhere to any rigid system; the heterogeneity of his techniques and methods corresponded to his policy of pragmatic expansionism. He used both free-trade and protectionist methods, both state subsidies and direct intervention; he both followed the trader and created for him areas in which he could operate. This wide variety of measures of assistance was directed however—as was Bismarck's economic policy in general—towards one permanent objective: that of assuring, securing and increasing economic advantages. Actual trading opportunities were to be defended, future possibilities kept open, and, last but not least, manufacturers were to be reassured of the state's readiness to assist them in overcoming the problems of the economic crisis. Expansion was a part of the anti-cyclical economic policy intended as an antidote to the pessimism of the depression years and as an incentive which would stimulate business. The intention always remained the same: to take pressure off the home market by extending foreign trade, to stimulate an economic revival and thereby to reduce the strain on the social and political system. "Our colonizing efforts are measures designed . . . to help German exports": such was Bismarck's summary of the functional value of the protectorates—they were "nothing more than an additional means of promoting the development . . . of German economic life."

The hope of obtaining trade outlets, initially in the Protectorates themselves but subsequently and more decisively in Central Africa, had been a dominant motive from the very start; it was to be the function of Germany's coastal possessions to secure access routes to these central areas. The question of markets was still of overriding importance in the 1880s, for it stemmed from the serious problems of overproduction in all industrial countries. It was not until the 1890s that the quest for raw materials assumed equal importance. Just as the chimera of an East Asian market of supposedly unlimited capacity had long fascinated businessmen, so, from the 1880s onwards, the illusion of a large Central African market exercised strong attraction.

In many places coastal acquisitions were only considered at all important insofar as they were able to provide controllable routes into Central Africa. When one considers how few of these hopes centered on the African interior were actually fulfilled, the history of European policy in Africa during the 1870s and 1880s can almost be described as the history of an illusion. This illusion, however, was of great importance in determining the actions of contemporaries.

It is not possible to say with certainty which of the three decisive economic considerations in Bismarck's imperialism was given priority at any one time: whether short-term or long-term factors or the need to restore business confidence. Taken together, however, these three considerations were certainly responsible for guiding Bismarck's anticyclical and foreign trade policies into the field of formal colonial rule. . . .

The early interventionist state was not only compelled by uneven economic growth gradually to extend state interference in its efforts to guarantee material welfare and social stability; it also realized, at a time when old political traditions were crumbling away and the charismatic authority of the Chancellor was more and more coming under attacks, that this wide field of economic policy provided new possibilities whereby governmental authority could be legitimized. Successful imperialist policies

promised in the same way to help to legitimize governmental authority, the basis of which was being questioned. Thus Bismarck's expansionist policies were from the outset Janus-faced [double-dealing]. Not only did he swim with the tide of his time; he also endeavoured with all the means at his command so to steer German political development on that tide, that it best met his needs. If from an economic point of view overseas expansion appears primarily as a necessary result of irregular economic growth, from the vantage point of domestic politics the active, guiding, indeed manipulatory role played by Bismarck is everywhere apparent, as he used expansion to electoral and parliamentary advantage, and for social-political and party-political purposes. On the one hand, his pragmatic expansionism followed the dynamics of the economic system and served as a means of providing an anticyclical therapy. On the other, it took over special domestic functions of integrating conflicting forces and of diverting attention from internal problems, thus contributing to the continuation of the Prusso-German "revolution from above. . . ."

The satisfaction that the national state had promised its subjects, the hopes of having all citizens live in harmony, enjoy equal rights and participate in the general prosperity—these hopes, which had been nurtured by the national-democratic, egalitarian aspect of nationalist ideology, were all revealed as illusions in the first period of serious economic fluctuations between 1873 and 1897. The harsh reality of the class structure of industrial society broke through to the surface of the new authoritarian state. . . .

The public agitation in favour of colonial expansion and the ideological consensus in favour of social imperialism and an export offensive were becoming unmistakably more widespread. The Chancellor recognized, as did the leading figures of this consensus, that imperialism could provide a new "vision of hope" (Fabri), "a distant, greater goal" (Hübbe-Schleiden), "a new, additional purpose" (v.d. Brüggen), or that it could at least be held up as a sort of "counter-utopia" in opposition to that of the democratic social-ist republic. When these advocates of expan-sion postulated "common economic in-terests in an overseas policy" as necessary to the "internal unity of Germany," they showed an awareness of the integrating effects of colonial expansion; again, it was "only through such expansion abroad . . . that the unity of our people . . . [could] be consolidated."

When Bismarck recognized the domestic possibilities of imperialism, he did not hesi-tate to exploit them. The ideological con-sensus showed him that some of the neces-sary prerequisites were fulfilled: the en-thusiasm for colonies was sufficiently wide-spread; its potential appeal, at any rate, was promising enough to act as a rallying point and to make it worthwhile turning to the electorate on this issue; it also gave sufficient scope to illusions and fears for a well-aimed propaganda to be able—with at least the appearance of credibility—to represent the decision to bid for colonies as a decision of fundamental importance; last but by no means least, however, it was able to perform the function of diverting attention from internal problems. The critical state of af-fairs during the period of depression after 1882 was particularly favourable to the growing emphasis on the domestic-political functions of the enthusiasm for colonies. . . .

From the spring of 1884 onwards Bis-marck began to guide the flood of colonial enthusiasm on to his own electoral mill. Fear of the Socialists had been exploited in previous elections (1877, 1881) as a means of integration; now the colonial fever was used in the same way. It was used on three different levels: first, against individual Deputies, in particular against the leading representatives of the political opposition like Eugen Richter and Ludwig Bamberger; second, against one or several groups of "Reichsfeinde," particularly against the Progressives; and third, against a foreign power, in this case Great Britain, in much the same way as Catholicism, the Socialist International and, in 1887, France were designated as opponents of the Reich. In each case the objective was to produce an effect beneficial to the government's poli-cies, putting out in the cold opponents at home and abroad. . . .

One aspect of German imperialism be-fore 1890 is the fact that Bismarck's over-seas policy in the broad sense—from the promotion of trade and exports to the acquisition of formal empire—was following the expansive tendencies of the German industrial state: this seemed to be necessi-tated by contemporary circumstances and by the requirements of the socioeconomic system. At the same time, however, it served to assert the supremacy of the traditional ruling elites and to preserve the hitherto protected social hierarchy and authoritarian power structure. This social and domestic side of imperialism, this primacy of the domestic political constellation, which was in these years under the most severe pressure as the result of the worldwide economic fluctuations, should probably be considered the most important of Bismarck's motives. Here was the juncture, as it were, where the tradition of the Prussian "revolution from above," continued by bonapartist methods appropriate to the time, was transformed into the social imperialism of an advanced industrial state, open for its part to all the social upheavals and economic fluctuations brought about by advanced capitalism.

Under this head the policies of the "conservative alliance"—the "landowner-industrial condominium directed against the proletariat" (E. Kehr), which had been deliberately pursued since the middle of the 1870s—the policy of protective tariffs, Puttkamer's handling of the bureaucracy, plans for the establishment of monopolies, the anti-Socialist law and the social policy: all these steps, together with the tentative anticyclical policy and the first measures of the interventionist state in the spheres of foreign trade and imperialism belong to one and the same socioeconomic and, above all, political context, as Bismarck sought by a wide variety of means not only to curb and restrain the dynamics of the industrial world, but also to exploit them as a means of preserving the status quo inside Germany. All these efforts show facets of the same labour of Sisyphus: ensuring and reinforcing the politically and socially threatened position of the ruling classes, as well as Bismarck's own autocratic position at the peak of the pyramid of power. He himself was clearly aware of this context. Again and again he described in his impressive language the defensive function of these measures for the benefit of the socially conservative, authoritarian state. He remained aware of the fact that the *Kaiserreich* of 1871 was a very precarious structure. Above all he considered that the continued existence of this *Reich* could be permanently assured only if the authority of the traditional and privileged ruling class were preserved, with the assistance of a compliant conservative bureaucracy and a military machine independent of parliament and run on semi-absolutist lines. He viewed with profound antipathy the spectre of possible future parliamentary and democratic rule. Perhaps he secretly felt that the situation was hopeless; but as long as it was possible, he thought defense against an inexorable fate worthwhile, regardless of the cost to society as a whole. Holstein, in spite of his increasing criticism of the Chancellor, admitted that only Bismarck would "accomplish . . . the greatest of all tasks, that of holding back the revolution."

Bismarck sought to extend the life span of the old authorities and structures by bonapartist, and ultimately by social imperialist methods. If one views imperialism as an integral part of this struggle of Bismarck's to defend his idea of the social order and his own power position, and if one also views the ultimate basis of this policy as the "stabilization" of the social order of the *Reich* of 1871, then one can understand his statement made to Ambassador Münster in London that "for internal reasons, the colonial question . . . is one of vital importance for us." It is well known that Bismarck was very reticent in his use of the terms "question of vital importance" and "vital interests." If he did decide to express the matter in those terms, then it was because he ascribed such an important domestic function to imperialist policies that he viewed "the position of the government at home as being dependent on [its] success." In 1886 Herbert V. Bismarck declared on his father's instructions that it had been "this concern for domestic politics" which had "made it essential for us" to embark upon formal colonial expansion, "since all those elements loyal to the *Reich* have the keenest interest in the success of our colonizing efforts. . . ."

Thus his overseas policy was also a component of Bismarck's policy of preserving the status quo in state and society: it held out the prospect of economic advantage, and acted as a sort of tension-conductor.

Jean-Louis Miège

POPULATION PRESSURES

Jean-Louis Miège (1923-   ), professor of history at the University of Provence, has written at great length on imperialism. Among his works are a four-volume history of Morocco and Europe, a text on European expansion, and one on Italian imperialism, from which this selection is taken.

Miège sees in overpopulation and in the fear of demographic developments the roots of Italian imperialism. He considers the thought of several leading journalists, publicists, statesmen and, lastly, labor leaders. With colonies Italy would have Italian soil on which to relocate a population that was considered too large, either because of absolute numbers or because various regions, especially the South, were unable to support the population.

FROM 1870 on, Italian emigration increased and, at the same time, became increasingly the subject of public concern. Information on emigration was not systematically collected until 1869; only in 1876, as a result of the efforts of the Ministry of Agriculture and Commerce, were annual statistical tables published.

Until the 1880s the average yearly departures numbered between 110,000 and 120,000 people; after 1880 the number increased and hovered around 155,000. More important than this increase in emigration, however, was the increase in permanent departures. In the decade 1869-1878 permanent emigration represented only a sixth of those leaving, a yearly average of 19,000; in the period 1879-1886 they represented between a third and a half of all those leaving, a yearly average of 60,000. The number of emigrants who left without the hope of returning had thus tripled in a few years. Moreover, southern Italy played a growing role as the source of emigration.

People from Basilicata, Calabria, Abruzzo, and Sicily provided a growing number of emigrants, most of them leaving for good. These new developments in Italian emigration led to several consequences. Around the world, large groups of Italian migrants formed. These colonies of people without a flag were located mainly in Latin America, but were also in North Africa, from Egypt to Morocco.

Italian public opinion was concerned about these departures and the fate of these transplanted minorities. Beginning in 1874, the writings of Carpi drew attention to the problem. His solution was the acquisition of colonies. From then on, that theme appeared more and more frequently. The Milanese paper, the *Emigrante,* constantly demanded that colonies be acquired to provide an outlet for emigration; this would spare the mother country the loss of these Italians on foreign soil. D. de Amici's work, *Sull'Oceano,* revealed to the general public the human drama of the emigration—"this

From Jean-Louis Miège, *L'Impérialisme colonial italien de 1879 à nos jours* (Paris, 1968), pp. 31-33, 41-45, 82-87. Reprinted and translated with the permission of the author.

wandering misery," which, from Genoa to Montivideo, carried away "the lost sons" of Italy.

The statesmen who had united Italy were particularly sensitive to the emigrants' suffering. That Italy, barely reunited and restored, had to be abandoned, seemed at once cruel and antithetical to the *Risorgimento*. They wanted a national emigration to lands that had become Italian. This desire reinforced the "imperialist themes" latent in the unification movement. . . .

Emigration suddenly increased in the years 1886 and 1887. For the three years 1884 through 1886, departures averaged 157,000 a year; in the following three years, it averaged more than 241,000. In 1886, permanent emigration exceeded for the first time temporary emigration. By 1888, two-thirds left without returning.

Population growth and the extent of emigration . . . became the main argument in favor of expansion in 1880. Crispi, in his speech of June 1889, affirmed that Italy needed a colony as a place to send "its excess rural population." Enrico Corradini used similar arguments stressing the over-population of Italy; he insisted that the sons of Italy must not be lost to foreign lands, but should flourish on Italian soil.

These themes became stronger as Italian emigration increased.

Italian Emigration

Year	Permanent Departures	Temporary	Total
1881	46,607	94,225	135,832
1882	65,748	95,814	161,562
1883	68,416	100,685	169,101
1884	58,049	88,968	147,017
1885	77,029	80,164	157,193
1886	85,355	82,434	167,829
1887	127,748	87,917	215,665
1888	195,993	94,743	290,736
1889	113,093	105,319	218,412
1890	104,733	112,511	217,244
1891	175,520	118,111	293,631
1892	107,364	116,248	223,667
1893	124,312	122,439	246,751
1894	105,455	119,868	225,323
1895	169,513	123,068	293,181

Emigration stimulated a double effort: on the one hand, to prevent the loss of national identity among the expatriates and, on the other, to make sure that they emigrated to areas where large groups of Italians were living already. The first efforts came from the Catholic hierarchy. In 1887, Monsignor Scalabrini founded the *Pia Società dei missionari di S. Carlo,* which was designed to aid Italian emigrants in America. Pope Leo XIII was also interested in the question; in 1887, he invited Bonomelli to direct an institute for priests for the Italian missions in Brazil. . . .Other religious institutions were founded in the following years to provide aid for the expatriates. . . .

The term "the emigration of the desperate" clearly revealed the general economic crisis of the 1890s, which affected all regions: Venice [in the North] sent 85,000 people to America in 1888. The crisis was worse in the South, however. The European agricultural depression, the system of land tenure with its very large estates, and the phylloxera epidemic affected the South more than other regions, increasing the misery of the peasants and leading to brigandage and uprisings. Africa appeared as a solution to the land hunger of the southern peasantry. The only other alternative was extensive land reform, which the Italian government found politically impossible to envisage. The attraction of Africa was thus partly tied to the southern question. Crispi's speech in Palermo on October 14, 1889 connected the need for colonies with the growth of population and land hunger. Increasingly, the accent would be on the land available through colonization, and the two questions—colonies and the southern question—became interconnected. It became commonplace for most supporters of colonies to come from the South: Mancini, Crispi, San Giuliana, and many others all came from there. The first movement in favor of expansion had come from the middle classes of the North in the years from 1878 to 1882. The second development, in the 1890s, found the industrialists of the North reluctant, if not hostile, toward African expeditions, while the middle classes of the South favored them. Beside the agrarian question, other motives for colonialism existed, such as the spirit of adventure, the hope of increased trade, and the idea of employment in the colonial administration. Southerners expected such developments to be particularly profitable to them. . . .

The movement of emigration grew to such an extent that it radically changed in meaning. The number of emigrants, which had averaged 250,000 per year between 1890 and 1895 (with a high of 293,631), rose to 353,000 in 1900 and in 1905 reached close to 788,000, having more than tripled in ten years. The rate stabilized between 1906 and 1910 at an average of 650,000, making a total of more than 10,000,000 emigrants for the years 1895-1915. . . .

The example of the newly enriched "Americans" stimulated a growing desire for expatriation as the road to wealth. Emigration seemed both a necessity and a possible answer to the worsening crisis of the South, whose overpopulation was as much due to economic and social factors as to demographic ones. Emigration was recognized as a "national fact" and the major problem of the day. The government felt it had to intervene and decided to control the issuing of passports. The General Commissariat for Emigration was founded.

Nationalists keenly felt Italy's hemorrhage of manpower as well as the humiliation of the expatriates as the sub-proletariat of richer countries. They applauded when Giolitti suspended emigration to Buenos Aires because of abuses against Italians in Argentina. They were concerned about the loss of national identity that Italians experienced abroad and argued for settling them in Italian territories. Senator Nobiliti-Vitelleschi, in a widely noticed article in the *Nuova Antologica* (1902) stressed that "the only easy, useful, moral, or enriching emigration is emigration carried on under the national flag, preserving our nationality, obeying our laws, and making fruitful the soil which is part of our motherland." In 1908, the first Congress of Italians Abroad had shown the influence of these millions of

emigrants and the use that could be made of them, by enlisting them in the cause of a colonial ideology. The second congress, also organized by the Italian colonial institute, met in Rome in June 1911. Opened in the presence of the King, the President of the Senate, the President of the Chamber, and the ministers, it brought together 354 delegates from all over the world, who met in six geographic groupings. The Congress coincided with the fiftieth anniversary of Italian unification and celebrated the greatness of being Italian. The "voice of millions of workers scattered through the world" was interpreted not only as a call for preserving ties with the mother country, but for expansion as well. The press gave great play to the meeting of the congress, which also won support from the working class. Thus, a new group now celebrated colonialism—the left wing and union groups. Influenced by the continued emigration and by the recession of 1907-1908, some demanded an imperialism that was "national and proletarian." This trend also existed in other European countries, in the social imperialism of the Fabians in England and of Renner in Germany. But the particular conditions in Italy gave it special characteristics. Proletarian support for Italian imperialism developed at this time. Two issues induced unions to embrace nationalism and a colonial ideology: the southern question and emigration. . . .Deeply swayed by ideological, political, and emotional values, public opinion ignored that Tripoli was economically without value. The occupation of Libya had become an *idée fixe* in Italian politics. After 1908-1909, there was a consensus favorable to annexing it. . . .

In an interview given to the *Giornale d'Italia* on April 13, 1902, Antonio Labriola revealed the extent to which Italian social imperialism was affected by a nostalgia for a united Mediterranean world [under Italian control] and concern for finding a solution to the emigration problem. Labriola, after deploring the Italian government's missed opportunity to occupy Tunis and Egypt, affirmed the need to take Tripoli. A good use of capital would make this territory suitable for emigration. The first nationalist congress, held in Florence in 1910, revealed the popularity of expansionism as the solution to emigration. It was a solution accepted by both nationalists and certain union leaders. . . .

The works of Scipio Sighele, *Il nazionalismo e i partiti politici* (1911), of G. Piazza, *La nostra terra promessa* (1911), and of Enrico Corradini, *L'Ora de Tripoli* (1911) spread colonial propaganda. They proclaimed that Italy "must embark on imperialism so that it can breathe," that "the solution to emigration is the conquest of Tripoli," and that "the occupation of Tripoli will be the start of Italy's spiritual rebirth,"

profitable to the middle classes and even more so for the proletariat. "The Italian nation must overcome its history. . . .A new period must begin, that of the rebirth of the Italian nation. . . .The occupation of Tripoli will be the first act of this *Risorgimento*. . . . To resolve the problems of the South and to occupy Tripoli are not opposite acts, but rather two convergent acts. . . ." The Libyan adventure seemed the first event to capture the enthusiasm of all classes in the country. It convinced them that "the nation would definitely be formed, and that Italy was becoming a reality for all people." This exaltation coincided with the anniversary of the unification. The *Tribuna* observed that "nationalist fever was sweeping the country."

Pierre Guillen

BUSINESS, GOVERNMENT, AND IMPERIALISM

Pierre Guillen, author of *Germany and Morocco from 1870 to 1905* (1967) and formerly professor of contemporary history at the University of Rabat, Morocco, now teaches at the University of Grenoble.

In this selection he critically examines the relationship between business and government in regard to imperialism. Rather than finding businessmen pulling the strings, Guillen concludes that in the final analysis, it was the governments which were in charge and which manipulated businessmen to win increased political leverage in the rivalry between European states.

THE ROLE of interest groups in the colonial expansion of the last century was and still is the subject of controversy, for it comprises part of a much larger ideological debate on the role of material, economic, and financial factors in the unfolding of history. Depending on whether one attributes a decisive influence to these

factors or considers them as one of many explanations, business activities appear either as the "guiding force" or as only one of the forces contributing to the development of imperialism. As historical research advances and specific cases are analyzed in depth, it is possible to ignore *a priori* doctrinal arguments and establish a more

From Pierre Guillen, "Milieux d'affaires et impérialisme colonial," *Relations internationales*, No. 1 (1974), pp. 57-69. Reprinted and translated by permission from the author.

sophisticated view of a complex phenomenon. This essay has two goals. First, it explores the attitude of business circles toward imperial expansion. Did they always prove favorable toward colonial initiatives, seeing in overseas expansion a policy to benefit their overseas interests? Was the development of such interests their main preoccupation? Secondly, this essay studies the relationship between businessmen and government. To the extent that businessmen attempted to influence government officials, was their relationship dominant or subordinate? Did financiers and industrialists exercise an irresistible pressure and impose their views, or did they rather conform to the "advice" and "counsel" of governments, which used them to achieve objectives that had, above all, a political character?

The thesis that colonial expansion occurred under pressure from business interests rests on the following concept: the conquest of overseas markets is a necessary function of the development of the capitalist economy. Two historical moments are usually singled out: the great depression of the 1880s and the concentration of monopolies in the last years of the nineteenth century and the beginning of the twentieth—moments that correspond to colonial expansion. A cause-and-effect relationship is seen between these two developments.

During the great depression, businessmen are supposed to have seen colonial expansion as the means to assure themselves of new markets. This would provide a remedy for falling prices, overproduction, and the difficulties of selling goods in a capitalist world that had returned to protectionism. Under pressure from businessmen, England supposedly embraced imperialism, Jules Ferry engaged the Third Republic in overseas expansion, and Bismarck decided to provide his Reich with a colonial empire.

The explanation connecting imperialism with protectionism is no longer believed today. First, Great Britain remained faithful to free trade, and the colonial initiatives of the European powers had begun quite a bit before Germany and France adopted protectionist tariffs. Second, to claim a connec-

tion between the colonial expansion of this period and the fears of businessmen is to forget all the conquests that had occurred for decades before.

A distinction has often been made between the first part of the nineteenth century, characterized as generally hostile to colonialism and overseas enterprise, and the age of imperialism, beginning in 1870. This distinction is totally artificial. It is unnecessary to list the colonial activities in the earlier, so-called liberal era. In fact, European expansion overseas was a powerful movement throughout the century, regardless of the ups and downs of the European economy. Moreover, Europeans did not wait for the great depression to discover the advantage that colonies offered as an outlet for products and capital. It is sufficient to remember the writings of the British economist Merivale in 1840, the speeches in the Chamber of Deputies during the [French] July monarchy, and the ideas developed by publicists and theoreticians during the [French] Second Empire. Jules Ferry's celebrated formula is usually cited: "Colonial policy is the offspring of industry." But was Ferry the mouthpiece of French business interests and responding to their concerns, and was he yielding to their requests when he acquired colonies? The interpretation generally accepted today is that he attempted, in his speeches and writings, to justify his term in office after the fact. Thus, he used arguments that he thought would prove attractive to the public, given the prevailing economic difficulties. The accusations of profiteering made against him were politically inspired. There is no proof that his colonial policy was determined by important French capitalist groups.

The views of the Englishman Hobson and the Austrian Hilferding, adopted and further developed by Lenin, explain that the imperialism of the late nineteenth and early twentieth centuries was caused by an excess of capitalist accumulation that resulted from financial and industrial concentration. . . . Thus, the financial groups were seen as dominant; their interests were at the root of imperialism. Investment in backward countries appeared to be the best means of limiting the fall in profits that occurred as a result of the [excess] accumulation of capital. In addition, the search for raw materials at low prices had become the principal driving force of the monopolies. In their struggle to control fields of investment and access to raw materials competing groups saw the acquisition of colonies, which implied political control, as the only sufficient guarantee for their interests. Finally, the surplus profit coming from the excessive exploitation of the colonized countries allowed the monopolies to raise salaries in Europe, "to corrupt" a segment of the working class by attaching it to the middle class, and thus to avoid social revolution at home.

There is no lack of objections to this interpretation. As for the final argument, although some businessmen reasoned like Lenin (who, incidentally, quoted Cecil Rhodes in his support), others felt that internal investments were the best means of developing the economy, raising the standard of living and avoiding revolution. That seems to have been the point of view of the majority of bankers and industrialists in Sweden or in the United States, countries that in 1914 did not export capital and in which the workers' standard of living was considerably higher than it was in colonizing countries such as Great Britain and France. Moreover, was the financial groups' need to invest surplus capital overseas the basis of imperialism? The United States and Japan were not exporters, but rather importers of capital; nevertheless, they acquired colonies. Germany was barely able to invest outside of Europe (the problems of financing the Berlin-Baghdad railroad is the best-known example), because it had a restricted financial market. It was not the excess of capital that pushed German businessmen to establish themselves overseas. The "German" capital that was invested was to a large extent foreign. Finally, it appears financial investors have had a clear preference for developed countries or for newly independent countries, such as those in Latin America. On the eve of the First World War, more than two-thirds of the foreign capital investments of Germany, France and Great Britain were located in Europe and America. Investments in the colonies were very modest. Great Britain was an exception and invested in very special kinds of colonies, the Dominions, which gained the lion's share of the investments going to the British empire. And even in Britain's case, most of the capital it sent abroad went to independent countries rather than to the empire.

Looking at particular cases, one notices that the attitude of business interests toward colonial expansion differed. It is essential to realize that the world of business was not a single entity with common values. One group consisted of those who were directly interested in overseas trade: shippers, trading houses, and light industries exporting consumer goods. In general, this group was always favorable to colonization. The establishment of political sovereignty in regions where there was a network of firms, trading posts, and houses would protect their interests by eliminating foreign rivals; occupying the territory would force the natives to work on plantations, and would provide direct access to the markets of the interior. Moreover, the needs of military expeditions, the presence of troops and government employees, and the establishment of an administrative and economic infrastructure would all create profitable business opportunities. The roles of the Bordeaux interests in the colonial policies of Baron Portal under the Restoration, of Faidherbe in Senegal and in the expansion inland from the trading points on the Guinea coast, of the Marseille interests in the conquest of Algeria, and of the Lyons interests in the early establishments of a French presence in Indochina, have been demonstrated.

At the beginning of the twentieth century, businessmen in Marseille and Bordeaux played a leading role among those who clamored for the annexation of Morocco. In the same way, English merchants and manufacturers, seeing that their clients [abroad] did not perceive the advantages of commercial transactions, demanded and obtained the opening of markets—by force if necessary. In the Far East, in India, in sub-Saharan Africa, the interests of English commerce were already determining the policies of colonial expansion in the liberal period [early nineteenth century], as has been stressed by English historians. In Germany too, the business communities of Hamburg and Bremen, which had established interests on the coast of sub-Saharan Africa and in the Pacific, induced their chambers of commerce to take a favorable position on colonies and to use their influence with the government. In the 1880s, shipping lines and large commercial houses played a decisive role in the formation of the English and German chartered companies that agitated for the partition of black Africa.

While they demanded the growth of their nation's colonial empire, commercial interests also attempted to prevent the expansion of powers that might exclude all other foreign interests from their possessions overseas. . . .Because the French established protective tariffs in their colonies and systematically favored their compatriots' enterprises, English traders incessantly demanded that their government oppose French colonial efforts. This situation formed an important part of the Anglo-French rivalry in sub-Saharan Africa, Southeast Asia, Madagascar and Morocco. In Germany, the situation was similar. The repeated pleas of the German chambers of commerce paralleled the campaigns of shippers, exporters, and Lancashire cotton manufacturers against a French protectorate in Morocco between 1902 and 1904.

Although most business circles involved in overseas trade seem to have placed colonial expansion at the forefront of their preoccupations, banks and heavy industry did not share a common attitude. From the beginning of the nineteenth century, the large English banks certainly showed a growing interest in investing overseas; issuing loans and making colonial investments were among their principal activities. They also played a considerable role in the creation of large colonies (Canada, Australia, New Zealand, and South Africa) and in the extension of English domination over India.

It is more difficult to interpret the penetration of English and French banks in Tunisia and Egypt in the 1860s. If financial interests were later used as instruments of colonial intervention, can one claim that, from the start, financiers were pursuing anything other than simple profits on loans to the khedive and the bey, or that they thought of these loans as means by which to win total control over these countries? The question remains open.

In the 1880s, during the partition of black Africa and the Pacific, big capital was not particularly active. The colonial charter companies had difficulty in raising sufficient capital (which is why English and German charter companies were taken over by the state); the insignificant amounts invested in the newly acquired territories reveal the lack of interest of the banks and large industries in colonies. They considered the opportunities for economic exploitation in these countries to be limited; in both the short and longer term, the investments did not seem profitable. The *Banque d'Indochine,* for example, refused to invest in Madagascar as a result of a pessimistic report by a mission sent out by the large banks in 1890. In addition, the conquest and organization of the new territories meant large expenditures by the mother countries, which had to pay for the permanent deficits in the colonial budgets; that ran the risk of causing an increase in taxes and the absorption of capital that could have been invested more profitably and usefully [at home] . The large banks and industries, especially in France and Germany, held such a view. But one must be careful not to generalize. If the English and German capitalists showed little enthusiasm for West and East Africa, they were definitely interested in South Africa, whose mineral wealth stimulated their greed. And many financial and industrial groups in Belgium gave Leopold II support for founding the Committee on the Upper Congo.

At the turn of this century, it seems that banks abandoned their earlier hesitancy. With the passage of time, established overseas interests grew; the era of the slave trade and of slow and difficult penetration seemed past, to be replaced by great works of development offering prospects of higher profits than before. Another possible explanation is that bankers and great industrialists, invited to join associations and committees interested in overseas expansion, were infected by the colonial ideology of the commercial traders. Two examples can illustrate this process: Central Africa and Morocco. While big German financial and industrial capital had long neglected sub-Saharan Africa, at the beginning of the twentieth century it multiplied its initiatives and its daring projects in the Cameroons, Belgian Congo, Angola, and East Africa, and encouraged the development of a German *Mittelafrika.* Beginning in 1900, when Morocco, prey to an internal crisis, seemed incapable of resisting Europe, big capitalism in England, Germany and France—which until then had shown only an absentminded attention toward the country—immediately swung into action. The objective was to obtain contracts for loans, concessions for public works, and mineral rights through European governmental pressure on the Moroccan state. The French groups were among the most enterprising. By exploiting the sultan's financial embarrassment, they hoped to assure themselves of control over the country's whole economy. To win the French government's support for its plans, it mobilized the press and colonial circles, and intervened with members of parliament and cabinet ministers. From very early on, it appeared that big capital in England and Germany did not desire to compete with French capitalism, but rather wanted to see their right to a fair share of the booty recognized. This restraint had two causes. First, the London and Berlin money markets, hurt by recent crises, needed support from their Parisian counterpart. Secondly, a bargain was struck. English capitalists expected that in exchange for their conciliatory attitude in Morocco the French would lift their ban on the financial and economic plans elaborated in Egypt by the Cassel group with the support of Lord Cromer. The German banks and heavy industry wanted an understanding with the French banks and heavy industry in Morocco, in order to have a free hand in Turkey. These agreements were never challenged, regardless of the political evolution of the Moroccan question. Ignoring the protests of the commercial interests, English big capitalism allowed France to increase its control of Morocco; in spite of the clamor by the pan-German and colonial groups, German bankers and large industrialists persevered in their desire to collaborate economically with the French and demanded that the government of the Reich accommodate France politically.

From the Moroccan case, it is possible to make a generalization about the role business played in the colonial rivalry of the European powers. The sector tied to commerce exacerbated these rivalries because the nature of its activities made it more sensitive to struggles with foreign competitors. Commercial interests considered the intervention of the state necessary to gain and protect their position and saw this intervention, above all, as the means of getting rid of those who competed for the market. Banks and heavy industry, however, given the international character that big capitalism increasingly exhibited, believed that there was a certain commonality of interests beyond national differences; it was better to agree on a partition of interests overseas than to carry on sterile confrontations that only risked degenerating into expensive conflicts. . . .

Rather than pushing for the inclusion of new territories in colonial empires, big capital, at the beginning of the twentieth century, seems to have preferred delimiting zones of influence, spheres of interest, in countries that theoretically remained independent. Economic and financial penetration, without military conquest or the establishment of political sovereignty, presented numerous advantages. This method limited the risk of conflicts that could undermine developing economic interests and also minimized expenditures, which otherwise would have to be used to establish full control. Finally, it seemed preferable to treat with weak governments: when one was negotiating loans, concessions for public works, or mining rights it was relatively easy to win advantageous terms from the Turkish or Chinese government, but far more difficult to obtain them from a powerful colonial administration. The division of world markets into spheres of interest in the independent overseas countries seems to have been the policy adopted by big capitalism in the years preceding the First World War. . . .

To understand the nature of relations between business and government in regard to imperialism, one has to ask what both their objectives were. Were they identical? Above all, business circles sought profits, a good return, and safety for their investments. For governments, colonial expansion occurred partly as a general policy of pursuing the national interest and partly as a complex of contingencies dictated by foreign and internal policies. Some historians consider this distinction between the economic and political worlds as artificial, claiming that these were but two aspects of the interests of the ruling class. This belief assumes that there was always a convergence of objectives. Certainly, one frequently discovers this convergence in the colonial domain. But how should it be interpreted? When Jules Ferry decided on the expedition of Tunisia or Tonkin, he was responding to the desires of certain financial and economic interests. Should one conclude that he ceded to pressure from them? In reality Jules Ferry, as recent studies have shown, was following his conception of the national interest. . . .The policy followed by Delcassé, aimed at the establishment of a protectorate in Morocco, coincided with the desires of large French capital. But above all, what explains Delcassé's policies was the imperial vision that he and French colonialists had of a larger France, built around the Mediterranean. It was motivated by the desire to. . .reaffirm to other powers, France's place among the concert of nations. Bismarck's overseas initiatives were preceded by petitioning and lobbying from chambers of commerce, shippers, and large traders. But interests of policy and especially internal policy dictated his decisions. In the same way, the *Weltpolitik* of Wilhelmine Germany

was not only the realization of political demands made by economic groups. Rather, it arose from a general conception of the power relationship between great states and from the political desire to make Germany a great world power.

Government and business seem to have had converging interests and frequently cooperated overseas. Governments increasingly viewed the opening of markets, investing, and the establishment of firms overseas as essential to the dynamism of the national economy and as factors contributing to the power of the state. Economic competition in the world appeared as a modern form of the ancient national rivalries; industrial and commercial expansion appeared to be the essential basis of national greatness. Moreover, financial and economic penetration appeared to be the most efficient means of exercising influences, laying claims against possible rivals, and progressively preparing the way for political control. Instead of affirming that politicians put themselves in the service of business, it seems more accurate to say that the statesmen saw businessmen as useful tools for their policies. One has but to remember that while there were many convergences, there were also many conflicts between government and business.

One reason for conflicts was the existence of rival interest groups inside a country, each fighting for official protection. Placed in the position of arbiters, ministers attempted to establish a consensus, since the division of the business community could only compromise the national interest overseas. When such an agreement proved impossible, ministerial support for one group provoked the hostility of the other. In Morocco, Delcassé at first gave his interests to the projects of the Schneider group, which appeared to serve his interests best; the *Banque de Paris et des Pays Bas* then did everything possible to undermine the minister's efforts to provide financial aid to the Moroccan government. Dealing with those large banks, Delcassé then had to face the hostility of the Schneider group, which, abandoned by the minister, carried on its own policies in Morocco and frustrated the policies of the French government. Schneider welcomed German intervention in 1905 as an act of providence that restored all his lost opportunities. Another cause of conflict was the business interests' timing. Wanting to make profits as quickly as possible, they showed a haste that governments found untimely. Delcassé was long opposed to both Schneider and the Parisian banks, since their plans would have raised the suspicion of the great powers and prevented a diplomatic solution to the Moroccan question. In the years 1903-1904, the German government likewise discouraged the German groups that demanded concessions in Morocco, fearing that their activities would precipitate the entente between London and Paris.

The drawing up of concession and loan contracts also created a divergence of interests. Desiring maximum profits, business groups wished to impose very harsh terms; yet that would have infuriated the rulers of countries which the European governments were trying to ease into dependency. Such terms would have destroyed the fiction of "friendly" protection, which veiled the progressive political takeover, and would have led the rulers to seek the aid of other powers. The controversy between the *Banque de Paris et des Pays Bas,* on the one hand, and the Ministry of Foreign Affairs on the other in regard to the Moroccan loan in 1904 is a striking illustration of this trend. . . .

The historian must be wary of making any generalization. Imperialism was the result of a complex grouping of political and economic factors that were intertwined with each other; the importance of one or the other varied according to time and country. Business interests were far from forming a homogenous interest group; the value they saw in overseas expansion and the form they thought it should take varied according to era and group. If business circles and governments often appeared to be playing the same tune on different instruments, the sound of false notes was frequent enough to lead one to conclude that the melody was not inspired by the same motives. On one side was big capitalism, increasingly international in nature and bent on the exploitation of the world; on the other, the will to power of the great national states. When a choice had to be made, the business interests before 1914 generally lined up under the banner of nationalism, without, however, losing sight of their own interests.

II. POLITICAL ORIGINS OF IMPERIALISM

Carlton J. H. Hayes

NATIONALISM

Carlton J. H. Hayes (1882-1964), one of the leading American authorities on the history of European nationalism, taught at Columbia University until his retirement in 1950. His writings include, among other works, *Essays on Nationalism* (1926), *France, A Nation of Patriots* (1930) and *Nationalism as a Religion* (1960). The following selection reveals the many intellectual forces contributing to imperialism; Professor Hayes finds nationalism to be the mainspring of imperialist activities. He argues that nationalism, unleashed by intellectuals, was readily adopted by the masses and directed not only against European neighbors but also overseas.

I N 1870-1871 European colonialism appeared to be approaching its nadir. Gladstone was prime minister of Great Britain, and he was notoriously a "Little Englander." The provisional French government so slightly esteemed the colonies it had inherited that it offered them all to Bismarck at the end of the Franco-Prussian War if only he would spare Alsace-Lorraine. Bismarck spurned the offer, as he had recently refused Portugal's offer to sell him Mozambique. A colonial policy for Germany, he said, "would be just like the silken sables of Polish noble families who have no shirts."

A favorite explanation of why European imperialism turned abruptly within a decade from nadir to apogee, has been the economic. It was advanced originally by publicists and statesmen to win the support of business interests for imperialistic policies, and it received classical treatment at the time of the Boer War by John A. Hobson. Latterly it has been taken up by Marxian writers and integrated with their dogma of materialistic determinism, so that the argument now runs in this wise: Imperialism is an inevitable phase in the evolution of capitalism, a phase in which surplus capital, accumulated by the exploitation of domestic labor, is obliged by diminishing returns at home to find new outlets for investment abroad. Hence it seeks nonindustrialized areas ever farther afield where it may dispose of surplus manufactures, obtain needed raw materials, invest surplus capital, and exploit cheap native labor. The resulting "new imperialism," unlike the old, is not primarily a colonizing or a simply commercial imperialism, but rather an investing one in regions

From pp. 216-229 in *A Generation of Materialism 1871-1900* by Carlton J. H. Hayes. Copyright 1941 by Harper & Row, Publishers, Inc.; renewed 1969 by Mary Evelyn Hayes. Used by permission.

ill-adapted to European settlement. Conditions are alleged to have been ripe for it about 1880, when tariff protection restricted customary markets of European capitalists and impelled them to seek new ones.

Doubtless large-scale mechanized industry, with accompanying improvement of transportation facilities, did immensely stimulate an ever-widening quest for markets where surplus manufactures might be disposed of, necessary raw materials procured, and lucrative investments made. Nor can there be any doubt that by the 1870s, when industrialization on the Continent was beginning seriously to vie with England's, the quest was being as eagerly pursued by commercial and banking houses of Hamburg and Bremen, Marseilles and Paris, as by those of London and Liverpool. In Germany, for example, at the very time when Bismarck was disdaining the French proffer of colonies, his banking friends, Bleichröder and Hansemann, were helping to finance distant trade ventures of various Hanseatic firms—O'Swald's in East Africa, Woermann's in West Africa, Godeffroy's in Samoa and other South Sea islands. In 1880 some 335,000 marks' worth of German goods were shipped to West Africa alone, while 6,735,000 marks' worth of African products entered the port of Hamburg.

Yet the only novel feature of all this was a relatively greater importation of tropical and subtropical products and hence a special concern with Africa, southern Asia, the Indies, and Oceania. Surplus manufactures from industrialized countries of Europe, even after the imposition of protective tariffs, still found export markets principally within that Continent or in temperate zones outside, notably in America, Australasia, northern India, and the Far East. What actually started the economic push into the "Dark Continent" and the sun-baked islands of the Pacific was not so much an overproduction of factory goods in Europe as an undersupply of raw materials. Cotton grew finer in Egypt than in the United States, and with the partial cutting off of the latter's copious supply by the

American Civil War it was but natural that dealers in raw cotton should enter the Egyptian field and raise its yield ninefold during the next twenty years. Rubber was now needed also, and it could be gotten from the Congo and from Malaysia more cheaply and plentifully than from Brazil. Copra, with its useful oil, was to be had in the South Sea islands, and the Godeffroy firm at Hamburg made a specialty of going for it. Tin was essential for the new canning industry, and gold, for measuring the new industrial wealth; rich supplies of the former were obtainable in the East Indies, and of the latter in Guinea and the Transvaal. Sugar cane and coffee, cocoa and tea, bananas and dates, if not directly serviceable to industrial machinery, were very palatable to the enlarging European multitude that tended it.

But commercial expansion into the tropics was a novelty of degree rather than of kind and hardly suffices to explain the political imperialism of the '70s and '80s. This was inaugurated prior to any general resort to tariff protectionism in Europe, and prior also to any universal export of capital. Neither Russia nor Italy had surplus manufactures to dispose of or surplus wealth to invest; yet both engaged in the scramble for imperial dominion, the one with striking success and the other not. Germany exported little capital until after she had acquired an extensive colonial empire, and France secured a far more extensive one while her industrial development lagged behind Germany's. Great Britain had long had all the supposed economic motives for imperialism—export of manufactured goods, demand for raw materials, supply of surplus capital—and yet these did not move her in the '60s as much as they did in the '70s. On the other hand, Norway, whose ocean-borne commerce was exceeded only by Great Britain's and Germany's, remained consistently aloof from overseas imperialism.

Apparently the flag of a European nation did not have to follow its trade—or its financial investments. But once flag raising became common and competitive in Africa and on the Pacific, economic considerations undoubtedly spurred most of the European participants to greater efforts and keener competition in those regions. Then the tariff protectionism of Continental nations was applied, in one form or another, to their respective colonies, and the more colonies each one had the greater were its opportunities for favorable trade and investment and the closer it approached to the ideal of all-around self-sufficiency. And to prevent too much of the world from being thus monopolized by France, Germany, Italy, or any other protectionist power, Great Britain moved mightily to gather the lion's share into her own free-trade empire. In other words, neomercantilism, once established, had very important imperialistic consequences.

The fact remains, nevertheless, that the founding of new colonial empires and the fortifying of old ones antedated the establishment of neomercantilism, and that the economic arguments adduced in support of imperialism seem to have been a rationalization *ex post facto*. In the main, it was not Liberal parties, with their superabundance of industrialists and bankers, who sponsored the outward imperialistic thrusts of the '70s and early '80s. Instead, it was Conservative parties, with a preponderantly agricultural clientele notoriously suspicious of money-lenders and big business, and, above all, it was patriotic professors and publicists regardless of political affiliation and unmindful of personal economic interest. These put forth the economic arguments which eventually drew bankers and traders and industrialists into the imperialist camp.

Basically the new imperialism was a nationalistic phenomenon. It followed hard upon the national wars which created an all-powerful Germany and a united Italy, which carried Russia within sight of Constantinople, and which left England fearful and France eclipsed. It expressed a resulting psychological reaction, an ardent desire to maintain or recover national prestige. France sought compensation for European loss in overseas gain. England would offset her European isolation by enlarging and glorifying the British Empire. Russia, halted in the Balkans, would turn anew to Asia, and

before long Germany and Italy would show the world that the prestige they had won by might inside Europe they were entitled to enhance by imperial exploits outside. The lesser powers, with no great prestige at stake, managed to get on without any new imperialism, though Portugal and Holland displayed a revived pride in the empires they already possessed and the latter's was administered with renewed vigor.

Public agitation for extending overseas the political dominion of European national states certainly began with patriotic intellectuals. As early as 1867 Lothar Bucher, one of Bismarck's associates in the Prussian foreign office, published in the influential *Norddeutsche Allgemeine Zeitung* a series of articles endorsing and advertising the hitherto neglected counsels of Friedrich List: "Companies should be founded in the German seaports to buy lands in foreign countries and settle them with German colonies; also companies for commerce and navigation whose object would be to open new markets abroad for German manufacturers and to establish steamship lines. . . .Colonies are the best means of developing manufactures, export and import trade, and finally a respectable navy." The next year Otto Kersten, traveler and explorer, founded at Berlin a "Central Society for Commercial Geography and German Interests Abroad," with an official journal, *Der Export*. Simultaneously the "Royal Colonial Institute" was founded at London; and a brilliant young English gentleman, Sir Charles Dilke, returning from a trip around the world, published his patriotic and immensely popular *Greater Britain*. Two years later, in the midst of the Franco-Prussian War, the redoubtable Froude scored his fellow Englishmen in the pages of *Fraser's Magazine* for their blindness to imperial glories. In 1872 Disraeli practically committed the Conservative party in Britain to a program of imperialism, and in 1874 Paul Leroy-Beaulieu, dean of political economists in France and implacable foe of tariff protection, plumped for French imperialism in a "scientific" treatise, *De la Colonisation chez les peuples modernes*.

These were foretastes. Heartier fare was served immediately after the Russo-Turkish War and the Congress of Berlin. In 1879 Friedrich Fabri, a pious promoter of Christian foreign missions, asked rhetorically "Does Germany need Colonies?" and answered with a resounding "Yes!" Germany's surplus population, he argued, should have places where it could go and still buy German goods and share in the other blessings of German *Kultur*. Fabri was eloquently seconded in 1881 by Hübbe-Schleiden, a lawyer and sometime explorer in equatorial Africa, who now insisted that through imperialistic endeavors "a country exhibits before the world its strength or weakness as a nation." In like vein the historian Treitschke edified his student audiences at the University of Berlin with the moral that "every virile people has established colonial power."

In 1882 a frankly propagandist "Colonial Society" was formed in Germany through the joint efforts of a naturalist, a geographer, and a politician, while in France Professor Leroy-Beaulieu brought out a new edition of his classic with the dogmatic addendum that "colonization is for France a question of life and death: either France will become a great African power, or in a century or two she will be no more than a secondary European power; she will count for about as much in the world as Greece and Rumania in Europe." The following year Professor John Seeley published his celebrated Cambridge lectures on the *Expansion of England*. The book took the British public by storm. It sold 80,000 copies within a brief time and won for its author the warm discipleship of Lord Rosebery and a knighthood.

In 1883 the stridently imperialistic "Primrose League" was launched by Tory Democrats, and soon afterwards the more sedate "Imperial Federation League" by nationalistic Liberals. In 1883, also, was founded a "Society for German Colonization." And capping the academic contributions to the imperialist cause, Froude published *Oceana* in 1885, while Alfred Rambaud, historian of Russia and first occupant of the chair in contemporary history at the

Sorbonne, edited in 1886 a cooperative work on *La France coloniale*.

Already, statesmen were following the professors and proclaiming that commerce and investments should follow the flag. If Gladstone hesitated, Disraeli and Salisbury did not; nor did such "new" Liberals as Rosebery, Chamberlain, and Grey. Jules Ferry surely did not hesitate. Replying to parliamentary critics of his aggressive policy in Tunis and Tonkin, he marshaled in speeches from 1881 to 1885 all the professorial arguments: that superior races have a civilizing mission to inferior races; that an industrial nation needs colonial markets; that coaling stations are requisite for navy and mercantile marine; and that if France refrained from imperialism, she would "descend from the first rank to the third or fourth." Bismarck seemed to hesitate more than he actually did. He privately expressed sympathy with imperialist ambitions in 1876 and publicly backed them, at least in the case of Samoa, in 1879. By 1884-1885 he was persuading the Reichstag that colonies were vital to national economy. Colonies would mean the winning of new markets for German industries, the expansion of trade, and a new field for German activity, civilization, and capital.

Most simply, the sequence of imperialism after 1870 appears to have been, first, pleas for colonies on the ground of national prestige; second, getting them; third, disarming critics by economic argument; and fourth, carrying this into effect and relating the results to the neomercantilism of tariff protection and social legislation at home.

There were, of course, complexities in the imperialistic movement. Insofar as it was economic, it did not affect the "capitalist class" as a whole, but only particular business interests: exporters and manufacturers of certain commodities such as calico and cheap alcoholic beverages; importers of rubber, raw cotton, coffee, copra, etc; shipping magnates; some bankers, though a very small percentage of all; and those "parasites of imperialism," the makers of arms and uniforms, the producers of telegraph and railway material, etc. But these last did not "cause" imperialism, they merely throve on it.

Christian missions provided an important adjunct to imperialism. They spread and multiplied in the second half of the nineteenth century as never before, in part as a reaction, we have suggested elsewhere, to the prevalent materialism in Europe, and in larger part because of the immensely improved means of travel and communication throughout the world. A missionary might have gone his way, like a merchant, the one conveying spiritual and the other material goods to heathen peoples, without any thought of raising a national flag over them or subjecting them to European rule. Actually, however, missionaries like merchants lived in a nationalistic age, and many of them were quite willing, on occasion, to invoke the naval or military protection of their respective national states. Not a few of Europe's footholds in other continents were obtained as penalties for the persecution of Christian missionaries. Even where missionaries did not directly prompt the extension of European dominion, they frequently paved the way for adventurers who did; and stories published back home by them or about them stimulated popular interest in, and support of, imperial undertakings. About David Livingstone, for example, something like a cult grew up in England, so that when he died in the wilds of Africa on May Day, 1873, his body was borne with hierophantic solemnity all the way to Zanzibar and thence under naval escort to England, where finally it was deposited amid Britain's national heroes in Westminster Abbey on April 18, 1874. The year was that of Disraeli's accession to the premiership, and for the popular favor accorded his subsequent imperial activities, he should have thanked the dead Livingstone more than any live merchant or banker.

It was a time, too, when evolutionary biology was beginning to occupy a central place in European thought, when hundreds of naturalists, emulating Darwin, engaged in scientific expeditions to strange distant regions and furnished millions of ordinary stay-at-homes with fascinating descriptions of the extraordianry flora and fauna they had observed. Already in 1861 the Franco-American Du Chaillu had reported from Gabun in equatorial Africa his amazing discovery of the gorilla, which was readily imagined to be the "missing link" between ape and man. In 1867 he published an account of a race of pygmies he had found, and for years afterwards his pen poured out popular tales of African adventure. Meanwhile, in the early '70s Faidherbe was exploring upper Egypt,* Nachtigal was visiting Khartoum, De Brazza was following Du Chaillu into the hinterland of Gabun, Skobelev with notebook in hand was investigating the borders of Turkestan, Evelyn Baring (the later Lord Cromer) was describing the natural wonders of India, and Henry Morton Stanley was "finding" Livingstone for the New York *Herald* and an avid public, and then heading an Anglo-American scientific expedition into the vast Congo basin. Presently George Goldie was exploring the Niger country, Joseph Thomson was leading an expedition into east-central Africa, Harry Johnston was traversing Angola and meeting Stanley on the Congo, and Frederick Lugard, a young veteran of the Afghan War, was penetrating Nyasaland and Uganda.

Of these explorers, the majority had military training. Faidherbe was a French general, former governor of Senegal, and Skobelev a Russian general who was to win laurels in the Russo-Turkish War. Nachtigal was a German army surgeon, De Brazza a French naval officer. Cromer and Goldie and Lugard had all been British soldiers. As a group they were intensely patriotic, and they nicely combined with scientific interests a zeal to serve the political, economic, and military interests of their respective nations. They were prime promoters of imperialism, and most of them remained as proconsuls of provinces they charted and helped to appropriate.

Sheer love of adventure was a potent lure to imperialism. Africa in particular, by reason of the widespread advertising its

*This is an error; Faidherbe was exploring Upper Senegal in the 1860s. [Ed.]

marvels and dangers received at the beginning of the '70s, beckoned to bold and venturesome spirits in Europe, and some of the boldest became empire-builders in the grand style, in a few cases acquiring fabulous personal wealth, in all cases experiencing that sense of power which comes from great achievement. Stanley was patently an adventurer. He had no surplus goods to sell, no surplus capital to invest. He was a self-made man, if ever there was one. A Welshman by birth, with the original name of Rowlands, he ran away from home and school at an early age to find work in Liverpool, first in a haberdasher's shop, then with a butcher. When this grew tedious he worked his way across the Atlantic to New Orleans and fell in with a merchant by the name of Stanley, who adopted him. At the outbreak of the American Civil War he enlisted in the Confederate army, only to be taken prisoner at the battle of Shiloh; then, "with ready versatility he joined the Union army to fight against his former comrades-in-arms. Toward the close of the war he discovered a latent talent for journalism which, when peace returned, led him to Salt Lake City to describe the extraordinary customs of the Mormons, then to Asia Minor in search of thrilling adventure, then with General Hancock against the Indians, with the British against Abyssinia, and to Crete, and Spain." He went to central Africa in 1871 because he was sent, but he remained to build a huge empire for another and the queerest kind of adventurer—a man who was not self-made and who never set foot in Africa, but who was as hypnotized by African dreams as by female realities—Leopold of the Belgians, Leopold of the Congo Free State.

But the adventurer-imperialist *par excellence* was Cecil Rhodes, and his extraordinary career began by accident. A sickly youth, son of an Anglican clergyman and intended for the church, he was bundled off in 1870, for purposes of health, to an elder brother's farm in southern Africa. He arrived just when diamonds were discovered in the nearby Kimberley fields. He joined other diggers, dug more industriously and successfully, and within a year found himself wealthy and healthy. He returned to England for study at Oxford, but the study was desultory and he was soon back permanently in South Africa, adding gold mines to diamond mines, running Cape politics, projecting British sway the entire length of the continent up to Cairo, and doing much to realize it.

The star German adventurer was Carl Peters. Son of a Lutheran clergyman and graduate of the University of Berlin, he contracted imperialist fever on a visit to England and set out in 1884 in disguise and under an alias—he was still in his twenties—to build an empire in East Africa. His method was simple, and the results startling, even to Bismarck. By a judicious distribution of toys plus injudicious application of grog, he got twelve big black chieftains, within ten days, to make their X's on documents conveying to Germany a total of 60,000 square miles. But that was only a start. Peters kept right on enlarging German East Africa until an Anglo-German convention of 1890 set bounds to his activity.

Explorers and adventurers gave rise to a peculiar species of organizer and administrator, despotic and ruthless and most devotedly imperialistic. Peters and Rhodes were transmuted by the African environment into this species, and so too were Cromer in Egypt and Milner at the Cape. For the glory of themselves and their countries, such local potentates carried on without too much regard for merely economic considerations or for the international engagements of their distant home governments. They were on the spot and knew better than London or Berlin or any other capital what had to be done, and they usually did it in an expansive way.

The actual course of empire—the order in which distant areas were appropriated by European powers—was determined less by design than by chance. Murder of a missionary or trader and consequent forceful intervention might occur anywhere. In some instances, curiously frequent in Moslem countries, native rulers practically invited intervention by living far beyond their means and contracting debts which they were unable to repay. Such was the basis of European imperialism in Egypt, Tunis, Persia, and to a large extent in Turkey. For example, the Khedive Ismail of Egypt, a squat, red-bearded gentleman with a passion for ostentation and the externals of European culture, spent half a billion dollars in the twelve years after his accession in 1863, running up the Egyptian public debt from 16 million to 342 million dollars and continuing to borrow money from European bankers at ever more onerous rates. In 1875 he could only get a quarter of the face value of short-term bonds bearing 20 percent interest. In 1876 he sold his shares of Suez Canal Company stock to England, and consented to joint supervision of his finances by representatives of England, France, Italy, and Austria. Soon this control was narrowed to England and France, and in 1882 to England alone. No doubt bankers and investors egged on both the khedive to spend and the English government to collect, but a less prodigal khedive, and one more intelligently concerned with the welfare of his subjects, might have staved off foreign rule. The contemporary Mikado of Japan did.

Especially active in directing the course of empire after 1870 were the European colonists already settled in Algeria, South Africa, and Australasia. These performed the same function in the latter part of the nineteenth century as their prototypes in the America of the eighteenth century. French settlers in Algeria were more eager than the government at Paris to make all adjacent African lands French. British and Dutch settlers in South Africa had almost a psychosis about others getting anywhere near them, and from the former, rather than from London, came the main drive for British expansion northward. Australians and New Zealanders were continually pressing the home government to forestall alien seizure of South Sea islands.

In many instances European flags were hoisted as a sport—a competitive sport—with about the same indifference to economic motives as characterized the later planting of American and other flags on cakes of ice around the North or South Pole. As one reads of successive French flag raisings in oases of the Sahara and on coral reefs of the Pacific, one gets a lively impression that it was all *pour le sport.*

Some capitalists undoubtedly promoted imperialism, and more profited by it. But in the last analysis it was the nationalistic masses who made it possible and who most vociferously applauded and most constantly backed it. Disraeli and Joseph Chamberlain were good politicians as well as patriots, and with a clairvoyance greater than Gladstone's, they perceived that in a country where the masses were patriotic, literate, and in possession of the ballot, a political party which frankly espoused imperialism would have magnetic attraction for them. So it proved. An unwonted popularity attended the Conservative parties of Britain and Germany during the '80s and '90s. The masses, of course, had no immediate economic interest in the matter, and it would have required an extraordinary act of faith on their part to believe the predictions of imperialistic intellectuals that somehow, sometime, everybody would be enriched from the Congo or the Niger or Tahiti. Rather, the masses were thrilled and stirred by front-page news in the popular press of far-off things and battles still to come. They devoured the yarns of a Rider Haggard—he had been secretary to the governor of Natal in the '70s and he *knew* his Africa. They learned by heart the vulgar verses of a Rudyard Kipling—he had lived in India and been a chum of doughty, swearing British soldiers. And the sporting impulse which drew crowds to prize fights and to football and cricket matches, evoked a whole nation's lusty cheers for its "team" in the mammoth competitive game of imperialism.

Into the imperial-mindedness of the masses, scarcely less than into that of Rhodes or Peters, Ferry or Chamberlain, fitted neatly the preaching of Darwinian sociology, that human progress depends upon struggle between races and nations and survival of the fittest. Obviously most eligible of the "fittest" were the white peoples of Europe, who therefore owed it to science as well as to civilization (and religion) to

establish their supremacy over inferior populations in all other continents. Which of
them would ultimately be adjudged the
absolutely fittest would depend on the
outcome of conflict among themselves as
well as with lesser breeds. This preaching
justified competitive devotion to duty. It
was summarized by Kipling at the close of
the generation (1899) in his famous lines:

> Take up the White Man's burden—
>   Send forth the best ye breed—
> Go bind your sons to exile
>   To serve your captives' need;
> To wait, in heavy harness,
>   On fluttered folk and wild—
> Your new-caught, sullen peoples,
>   Half-devil and half-child.
>
>   From Rudyard Kipling,
>   "The White Man's Burden."

Jean Stengers

THE STATESMAN AS IMPERIALIST

Jean Stengers (1922-   ), professor of history at the University of
Brussels, is one of the leading historians of Belgian expansion. Most of his
books have dealt with Belgian activities in the Congo. Stengers reveals that
the impetus of Belgian expansion was the desire of King Leopold II to
provide himself with a colony. Searching the globe for a suitable place, he
decided on this central African country. While Stengers considers Leopold's actions to be original, other European statesmen were equally en-
amored of empire, although few had such an unmixed motive.

L EOPOLD II's ideas about colonies
shaped his imperial policy. Taking
into account Belgium's industrial
character Leopold proclaimed that the country should direct its main effort toward
funding new outlets for its manufactures.
The safest and most stable outlet for products and capital was, of course, a colony.
Hence, he believed that it was in Belgium's
interest to create a colonial domain. This is
the thought that the young Duke of Brabant
forcefully expressed from 1860 on.

The colonial doctrine that Leopold II
articulated at age twenty-five endured
throughout his life. It inspired his whole
policy. In this his policies were original, for
if one surveys nineteenth-century European
colonization (at least until the years
1880-1885), one notices that doctrine, compared with circumstances, played a minor

From Jean Stengers, "La Place de Léopold II dans l'histoire de la colonisation," *Nouvelle Clio,* Vols. I and
II (1949-1950), pp. 517-522, 524, 527-528, 533, 536. Reprinted and translated with the permission of
the author.

role. European colonial expansion from 1800 to 1885 was hardly ever guided by theoretical considerations. British or French statesmen who conquered colonies did have more or less well-developed ideas on the utility of colonies, but the ideas themselves did not determine their actions; rather, circumstance and contingency played the decisive role in nearly all cases. Colonial conquest was almost always decided by practical considerations or necessities. The government that carried out the conquest did so to assure the security of nearby colonies, to defend its nationals against a native ruler, to prevent a foreign power from installing itself in the country, or simply to achieve an easy and quick victory that would increase its popularity. Thus, nineteenth-century colonialism appears overwhelmingly to have been dictated more by conditions than by theory. Leopold II was the exception to this rule. All his policies were based on his doctrine; no particular circumstances led him to found colonies. He entered the race for empire simply because that was his program. This makes him unique.

Although Leopold's motives were sensible and well-reasoned, his actions were of an impetuosity that owed little to reason. General Strauch, one of the earliest and most active of Leopold's collaborators, observed toward the end of his life that the king had thrown himself into the Congo adventure with "no previous study of the question." Leopold's early attempts at colonizing the islands of the Pacific, establishing himself in Northern Borneo, buying the Philippines, and making proposals to both Holland and Portugal bring Strauch's comment to mind. It is clear that the king's efforts were not guided by any knowledge of the resources of the countries he wanted to acquire. He wanted a colony, sought one in every direction, and was ready to seize the first one he could find. And after this obsessive quest, he pounced on the Congo. That was the decisive moment and it is worth analyzing the situation.

Leopold sent Stanley on an expedition in the beginning of 1879. Less than four years earlier, the region that the king of the Belgians wished to conquer had been officially offered to England. While navigating the upper basin of the Congo River in 1874-1875, the English explorer Cameron had concluded treaties with the native chiefs, thereby granting England protectorate powers over the land. Before leaving Africa, Cameron had laid claim to the Congo basin in the name of his sovereign. Upon his return to London in 1875, he eagerly submitted his treaties and proclamation to the British government. The Foreign Office disdainfully ignored them. British public opinion proved equally indifferent when Stanley, who had remained a good British patriot, attempted to raise interest in the large territories he had discovered. England remained uninterested in Central Africa.

The general view was that these areas were of such small economic value that they could not be exploited profitably. The Portuguese foreign minister seems to have been sincere, when, in 1884, he told the Belgian representative in Lisbon that an enterprise in Central Africa, such as Leopold's, would never be profitable, or at least that it would not pay off for many years. That was certainly the general feeling among political circles in Europe.

Leopold II's initiatives were not due to his possessing any additional information for he knew no more than his contemporaries. Like them, he based his knowledge on Stanley's works. Stanley had brought back from his great expedition only vague information. He was an explorer of extraordinary energy but limited scientific ability; while descending the [Congo] River he had been unable to make a scientific analysis of the wealth of the areas he was crossing.

Leopold thus had no reason to believe that the Congo was rich. He seized this practically unknown region simply because he was motivated by faith in empire. He wanted a colony and took whatever he could find. The rest was a matter of luck, and fortune assured that the region he annexed had valuable resources. These prodigious resources were twofold: those of present-day Kasai, Katanga or Kilo-Moto [minerals], and the resources that could be exploited in the Congo immediately. To understand the importance of the latter it is sufficient to remember what the resources of the Congo were, compared with those of a colony like German East Africa. By 1907, when the Congo had been providing considerable profits for more than ten years, East Africa still depended on the mother country for 60 percent of its expenditures. The reason was that the Congo had an advantage absent in East Africa—rubber. Undoubtedly, without the rubber that the lianas of the equatorial forest immediately and abundantly provided, Leopold II, with his limited resources, would have faced catastrophe. He would have been unable to finance the Congo state while it was being developed economically. In the face of a permanent and hopeless deficit, he would not have been able to count on Belgium for help. But the god of chance smiled on Leopold. The mineral resources of the Congo, of which the king could know nothing, and its richness in rubber, which became apparent only rather late (1893-1894), appear as the double triumph of a lucky gambler.

The real gamble in the Congo was his decision to throw himself into the conquest of a vast and unknown area, and he did it with tenacity and a sense of purpose. Leopold II directed the political and commercial activities of the enterprise completely, keeping all the strings in his hands. This also indicates Leopold's originality, for in fact, in colonial history the great achievements are usually explained by the conjunction of two factors—the activities of the metropolitan authorities and those of the colonial officials and settlers. In addition to the initiatives of the metropole, there were nearly always the still more daring activities of Europeans in the colony. But in the Congo, there was no such conjunction. Everything came from Leopold. The king's agents in Africa, tightly controlled by their master, conformed to his will.

The king considered himself not only the sovereign of the Congo, but also as the proprietor, in the true sense of the word, of the Congo state and its territory. The texts show this. In a note of 1901 the king

defined himself as "the absolute uncontested owner of the Congo and its wealth." In reviewing the past, he wrote that "The king was the founder of the Congo state, he was the organizer, the owner, the proprietor, the absolute sovereign. . . ." The Congo was his, his creation, which he had developed with his money and labor; could he not say that he owned it? He had no hesitation about making such a claim, since his conception of colonies fit his description. His doctrine of expansion was economic. In his eyes, a colony was worthwhile essentially because of the economic advantages it offered the mother country; above all, the colony had to be a profitable commercial enterprise. Of course, the notion of a commercial enterprise reminds one of the idea of property. It was the great capitalist, the contemporary of Rockefeller and Carnegie, who declared that he owned the Congo as Rockefeller owned Standard Oil or Carnegie his metal factories.

In his ideas of the relationship between colonies and a mother country, the king was profoundly influenced by the theories of the ancien régime: a colony, in his opinion, was made for the mother country and was to serve the interests of the metropole. He once referred to the Congo, in a slip of the tongue, as "a milk cow." The expression may have been excessive, but it certainly reflected his thinking.

At that time, Leopold presented himself as a philanthropist, as a totally disinterested man, trying to found what one might call an "ideal colony." His rhetoric was systematically designed to win the sympathy of the civilized world for the future Congo state. Leopold II attempted to win the support of his contemporaries by promising the suppression of the slave trade and of cannibalism. His strongest appeal was his promise to open the Congo, according to the formula he enjoyed using, to the "commerce of all nations." Essentially this meant serving the interests of white nations. While Leopold was preoccupied with presenting himself as an ideal colonizer, he did not put primary emphasis on the needs of the natives, who are today considered the main object of concern. These commercial values typified both the king and his era.

"The duty of a sovereign," he declared on the eve of his death, "is to enrich his

nation." That was how he perceived his life's work: by acquiring the Congo for Belgium, he had fulfilled his duty and enriched his country.

Ronald Robinson and John Gallagher

EMPIRE AS WORLD STRATEGY

Ronald Robinson (1920-   ), Fellow of Balliol College and Beit Professor of the History of the British Commonwealth, Oxford, and John Gallagher (1919-   ), Vere Harmsworth Professor of Imperial and Naval History, Cambridge University, together wrote the influential *Africa and the Victorians: The Official Mind of Imperialism* (1961). The theme of that book and of this selection is that most of Africa, rather than being partitioned between France and Britain for its intrinsic value, was a pawn in a struggle for the control of Egypt. With its large possessions in India, Britain desired to secure the Suez Canal and thus occupied Egypt. Then, obsessed with the safety of Egypt, Britain moved southward to safeguard the headwaters of the Nile. France, which also aspired to control Egypt, was humiliated by Britain's action and attempted to force a British evacuation by encroaching on the Nile. In the process France acquired considerable real estate.

Robinson and Gallagher view strategic interests as having shaped the timing and the direction of European imperialism in the late nineteenth century.

SINCE THE nineteenth century began, the Europeans had been strengthening their hold over those parts of the world selected during the era of mercantilism. Australasia, India, Southeast Asia, above all the Americas—they were either temperate regions peopled with white immigrants or tropical countries already under white rule. Step by step the mode of white

expansion has altered: liberalism and industrial growth shifted the emphasis away from colonies of formal empire to regions of informal influence. But whatever the form it had taken, the groundwork of European imperialism had been truly laid long before the cartographical exercises in partition at the end of the century. Africa was the last continent to win the interest of the strate-

From Ronald Robinson and John Gallagher, "The Partition of Africa," *New Cambridge Modern History,* Vol. XI, *Material Progress and World-Wide Problems: 1870-1898,* pp. 593-595, 597-602, 609-611, 613, 615-617, 622-624, 626-629. Copyright © Cambridge University Press, 1962. Used by permission of Cambridge University Press.

gists of expansion; it seemed to them that here they were scraping the bottom of the barrel.

Dividing Africa was easy enough for the Europeans. They did it at that moment in history when their lead over the other continents was at its longest. Economic growth and technical innovation gave them invincible assurance and force. Their culture and political organization gave them a carrying power to match their iron ships and high-velocity guns. That Europe had the capacity to subjugate Africa was self-evident; but had her rulers any firm wish to do so?

Twenty years were enough to see the continent carved into symmetries devised by the geometers of diplomacy. By the end of the century only Morocco and Ethiopia were still independent, and their turn was coming. But the statesmen who drew the new frontier lines did not do so because they wanted to rule and develop these countries. Bismarck and Ferry, Gladstone and Salisbury had no solid belief in African empire; indeed they sneered at the movement as something of a farce. A gamble in jungles and bush might interest a poor king such as Leopold II of the Belgians, or a politican on the make such as Crispi, but the chief partitioners of the 1880s glimpsed no grand imperial idea behind what they were doing. They felt no need of African colonies and in this they reflected the indifference of all but the lunatic fringe of European business and politics. Here their historians must follow them. For all the hindsight of social scientists, there was no comprehensive cause or purpose behind it. In all the long annals of imperialism, the partition of Africa is a remarkable freak. Few events that have thrown an entire continent into revolution have been brought about so casually.

Why then did statesmen bother to divide the continent? It used to be supposed that European society must have put out stronger urges to empire in Africa at this time; and all sorts of causes have been suggested to support the supposition. One and all, however, they suffer from a tiresome defect: of powerful new incentives there is remarkably little sign. . . .

Scanning Europe for the causes, the theorists of imperialism have been looking for the answers in the wrong places. The crucial changes that set all working took place in Africa itself. It was the fall of an old power in its north, the rise of a new in its south, that dragged Africa into modern history.

From these internal crises, erupting at opposite ends of the continent, there unfolded two unconnected processes of partition. That in southern Africa flowed from the rise of the Transvaal on its gold reefs, from a struggle between colonial and republican expansion that reached from Bechuanaland to Lake Nyasa. It eventually drove South Africa into the Jameson Raid and the Boer War. The second crisis was the breakdown of the Khedivate in the Egyptian revolution of 1879-1882. Their misdealings with this new protonationalism brought the British stumbling onto the Nile and trapped them there. This was crucial. It led to bad blood between them and the French in a quarrel that was to spread over all tropical Africa before being settled at Fashoda in 1898.

Hence Europe became entangled in tropical Africa by. . .internal crises. Imbroglios with Egyptian proto-nationalists and thence with Islamic revivals across the whole of the Sudan drew the powers into an expansion of their own in East and West Africa. . . . The last quarter of the century has often been called the "Age of imperialism." Yet much of this imperialism was no more than an involuntary reaction of Europe to the various proto-nationalisms of Islam that were already rising in Africa against the encroaching thraldom of the white men. . . .

The partition of the African tropics which began [in 1883] was not the result of the Tunisian mishap, or of Leopold's schemes and Bismarck's wiles, or of the squabbles of white merchants and explorers on the spot. What drove it on was the Suez crisis and the repercussions of that crisis.

A recognizably modern nationalist revolution was sweeping the Nile Delta by 1882; its leaders are much more familiar figures today than the proconsuls who put them down. The Egyptians were reacting against increasing interference over the past six years by Britain and France. Anxious to renovate the crumbling state on which their amicable dual paramountcy and their security in India and the Mediterranean in large part depended, they had acted with a high hand. At their behest, the Khedivate had been clothed in the decencies of constitutional monarchy, the army cut, and the landlords obliged to pay their dues; the khedive Ismail had been sent packing, Tewfik raised in his place and two-thirds of the revenue sequestrated to satisfy the bondholders. Small wonder that the Notables were using the constitution to break their foreign fetters. The mulcted peasantry was at the point of revolt. Muslim gorges were rising against Christians; the army had mutinied to recall dismissed comrades, and the pashas were defending their fiscal privileges in the guise of patriots ridding the country of the foreigner. By January 1882 all were uniting against the Anglo-French Financial Controllers and the khedive who did their will. The French consul reported that Tewfik had lost all prestige; the British that Arabi and his colonels had practically taken over the country. . . .

Here. . .was "an anti-European movement. . .destined to turn into fanaticism"; but this time it had the professional army at its head. Gladstone, then prime minister, anticipated "with the utmost apprehension a conflict between the 'Control' and any sentiment truly national, with a persuasion that one way or the other we should come to grief." "Egypt for the Egyptians [was] the best, the only good solution to the Egyptian question." This was true. But as the "union between [Britain and France] on that. . . question was the principal symbol" of their overall entente, both gave priority in the crisis to keeping in step. Each might grumble at going it together; neither desired to go it alone. The unpopularity of the Tunisian adventure was enough to deter Freycinet's ministry from another promenade in North Africa. Gladstone's Liberals, who had just retired from the Transvaal and Afghanistan and washed their hands of Tunis and Moroc-

co, still had their scruples about meddling abroad. Yet something had to be done. Clearly the ideal solution, the only one as Gladstone had said, was to come to terms with Arabi. This was tried. Paris offered him a paid holiday to study European armies; London tried to reconcile him to the khedive. But Egyptian feelings were too heated for Arabi to agree to the one condition that seemed indispensable: abiding by the Financial Control. So long as he refused this, the British feared a foreign thrust at the jugular vein of Suez, and the French feared Turkish intervention which would bring the aid of Islam nearer to their dissident subjects in Tunis and Algeria. On 6 January 1882 the joint note announced the conclusion of Gambetta, unwillingly subscribed to by Gladstone. The khedive must be supported and the Control upheld. What was not announced was the equally emphatic conviction of the two governments that landing an army in Egypt for this purpose would defeat its own object. Freycinet could not move because the Chamber was opposed, and so an invasion would hand Egypt to the British on a plate. Gladstone's cabinet too was in a dilemma. Intervening singlehanded would mean a breach with France. A joint intervention would give France a half-share in the route to the East. Granville at the Foreign Office listed the objections: "Opposition of Egyptians; of Turkey; jealousy of Europe; responsibility of governing a country of Oreintals without adequate means and under adverse circumstances; presumption that France would object as much to our sole occupation as we should object to theirs." The official case against going into Egypt was overwhelming. As Disraeli had said, "Constantinople [was still] the key to India, not Cairo and the Canal." At few times in the century had Anglo-French rivalry in the Mediterranean been so composed. Added to that, the late-Victorian pessimism about the possibilities of making English gentlemen of "Orientals" made another strong argument against conquering new Indias. All the plans therefore were for staying out and solving the problem from outside.

But effective as the arts of "moral influence" had been hitherto in bending pashas and mandarins to European whims, they were to prove worse than useless against Arabists, Mahdists and Boxers whose mass defiance signalled the political awakenings of Islam and the Orient. Instead of sobering the colonels and saving the Control, the pressures of gunboat diplomacy and the European Concert only added to the charismatic appeal of Arabi, *el Misr,* the "Egyptian." The Anglo-French naval demonstration of June [1881] provoked a massacre of Europeans at Alexandria. This destroyed Arabi's credit with the English Liberals, and although the French squadron sailed away, Beauchamp Seymour was allowed to bombard the Alexandrian forts to show that Britain at least was in earnest. This old-fashioned device proved the critical blunder, the point of no return. Arabi proclaimed a *jihad* against the British; rioting spread to the interior. According to the dogmas of strategy, if Suez was in jeopardy, it must be protected at any cost. According to Anglo-Indian orthodoxy, the *jihad* challenged imperial prestige throughout the Muslim East. Hence for Gladstone's ministers, "the question [was] no longer what form of intervention [was]...most unobjectionable, but in what form it [could] be most promptly applied." No chance of French or international cooperation was left. But in applying their conventional routine of threat and bluff to cow the Egyptians, the British had raised the stakes so high that now they had to win by any means. On 16 August Sir Garnet Wolseley and the redcoats landed on the Canal for another small colonial war. They routed the Egyptian army at Tel el Kebir, imprisoned Arabi and reinstated Tewfik. Gladstone's government pledged its word that as soon as the Canal was safe and Tewfik strong, it would bring the troops home and leave the Egyptians "to manage their own affairs."

There is no doubt that this is what the Liberals meant to do. Like the French in Tunisia, they simply intended to restore the old security through influence without extending their rule. The expedition was to be

a Palmerstonian stroke of the kind that had brought the Turk to reason in 1839-1841, and chastened the Chinese in two opium wars, the Ethiopians in 1869 and the Ashanti in 1874. Many months passed before they realized that, having rushed in, they could not rush out again; that they had achieved the occupation which above all they had wanted to avoid. By 1884 they had to confess privately that "the theory on which we orginally undertook [to go in]... however plausible, has completely broken down." The models for intervention proved as outdated as the Crystal Palace. From start to finish the British had miscalculated. They had gone to restore the *status quo ante Arabi,* and discovered that it no longer existed. They had come to restore a khedive and found him a cypher without the authority of British bayonets. And so they had gone in and they could not get out.

What first opened their eyes was another crisis in Africa. After Mehemet Ali had conquered the eastern Sudan for Egypt, the khedive Ismail had laid heavy tribute upon its people. At the same time, he had put down the slave trade, thus depriving them of their chief means of staving off the tax-collector or his bastinado. He had employed white governors to impose Christian ethics on his Muslim subjects. Detesting the imperialism of Cairo, the Sudanese struck back at the Egyptians once they had been disarmed by revolution and invasion. As so often in Muslim Africa, the liberation movement took the form of a puritan revolution against the religious latitudinarianism of the foreign ruling class. In 1881 the Mahdi, Mohammed Ahmad, began his preaching and the revivalist Dervish orders forged the politically discontented sheikhs and deposed sultans, slave traders and tribes, into an army and a state. At first the implications of the *Mahdia* were hidden from the British in Egypt behind a curtain of sands, until news came in November 1883 that the Mahdists had cut the Egyptian troops in the Sudan to pieces. Without soldiers or money, Tewfik could not hold Khartoum. There was no resistance left between the Mahdi and Wadi Halfa. Just as the British were handing back Tewfik a much qualified independence and withdrawing their troops from Cairo, the Mahdi's advance compelled them to stand in defense of the frontiers of Lower Egypt. At last the sinister truth dawned in London. As ministers complained: "We have now been forced into the position of being the protectors of Egypt." As with Arabi, so with the Mahdi, there was no chance of striking a bargain of the old mid-Victorian sort. Against fierce Egyptian opposition Gladstone ordered Tewfik to abandon the Sudan and stop the drain on his exchequer, while Gordon was sent to his death at Khartoum attempting the impossible. In enforcing the abandonment, Baring practically had to take control of the khedivial government, and the tighter he gripped it, the deeper the British became involved in its financial difficulties. By this time the unpopularity of the Egyptian fiasco matched that of the Tunisian affair in France. It was increasingly clear that Gladstone's ministry had made fools of themselves. They had hoped to set up an independent Egyptian government; but hampered by the *Mahdia,* the loss of the Sudan, the bankruptcy and the Control's unpopularity with the proto-nationalists, they found no Egyptian collaborators to whom they could transfer power with safety. Nor could they retire so long as the infuriated French refused to admit the exclusive paramountcy in Cairo which they claimed as their due reward. For if they left, the French would upset their influence, or the Egyptian nationalists or Sudanese invaders might upset the financial settlement, and all the dangers of the Suez crisis would arise again. . . .

The longer the British garrisons remained, the stronger grew the arguments for staying. By 1889 the "veiled protectorate" had become a necessity for imperial security in the world. As Salisbury said, "the appetite had grown with the eating." Sir Evelyn Baring and the Anglo-Indian officials who governed in the name of the khedive, brought from Calcutta to the Nile their professional distrust of nationalists. It became inconceivable that the Egyptians could be trusted to govern themselves. Arabist sentiment still smouldered. In taking over the country, the English had stopped its politics in a state of betwixt and between. Its obsolete Turkish rulers had fallen, but its rising liberal leaders had been put down. So Baring had to rule until native authority revived, but native authority could hardly revive while Baring ruled. If evacuation was impossible for internal reasons, it soon became impracticable on external grounds. Eventually the occupation drove France into the arms of Russia; and this combined menace in the Mediterranean, together with the further crumbling of Turkish power, enhanced Egypt's importance to Britain. After 1889 therefore, the resolution was to stay and keep the lid on the simmering revolution, rather than withdraw and invite another power to straddle the road to India. Henceforth England's statesmen were to be bewitched with the farfetched fancies of the Nile Valley strategy. To be sure of the canal and lower Egypt, they were to push their territorial claims up the Nile to Fashoda and from the Indian Ocean to Uganda and the Bahr-al-Ghazal.

On an Olympian view, the taking of Egypt might seem to have been the logical outcome of two great movements of European expansion since the end of the eighteenth century. One was the long buildup of British trade and power in the East; the other was the extension of Anglo-French influence which had so thoroughly disrupted Ottoman rule in Egypt and the Levant that the routes to the East were no longer safe. Certainly this long-term logic set limits to the problem. But what determined the occupation of Egypt in concrete terms was not so much the secular processes of European expansion as the Arabist and Mahdist revolutions against its encroaching mastery. When they baffled the customary informal techniques of France and Britain, it was too late to find any other solution but conquest and rule.

The shots of Seymour at Alexandria and Wolseley at Tel el Kebir were to echo round the world. It transpired in the end that their *ricochets* had blown Africa into the modern age. The onslaught on Arabi opened the long Anglo-French conflict over Egypt which more than anything brought on the division of East and West Africa. Up to the 1890s it was merely a partition on paper. The politicians in the European capitals at least intended it to go no farther than that. Hitherto they had ignored the clamor of their merchants, missionaries and explorers for advances in tropical Africa. They had done so with good reason. Communications were difficult; the tribes of the hinterlands seemed lost in chaos; there were grave doubts whether the African could be persuaded to work, or whether he could work at anything worth producing; prospects of trade or revenue seemed gloomy indeed. If governments had sometimes bestirred themselves to help private traders and sent frigates along the coasts to atone for the sins of the slave trade, such acts were not intended as commitments. Since large or stable authorities were few and far between, even the simplest methods of informal expansion worked badly in tropical Africa. Clearly then, this was no place for colonies. For decades before 1882, therefore, a gentlemen's agreement between the powers saw to it that the petty quarrels of their merchants and officials on the coasts did not become pretexts for empire.

But when Gladstone stumbled into Egypt that era ended. To the French, the veiled protectorate was the worst humiliation since Sedan. Their canal and the country which they had nursed since Napoleon's landing had been snatched away under their very noses. This broke the Liberal entente and kept Britain and France at odds for twenty years. Once in Egypt, moreover, Britain became highly vulnerable to continental diplomacy. To set Egyptian finances in order, she needed German support against French vetoes in the Debt Commission if her ministers were to avoid asking their critical Parliament to subsidize the khedive. By altering European alignments thus, the Egyptian occupation for the rest of the century gave the powers both incentive and opportunity to break the traditional understandings about tropical Africa. While Baring played the puppet-master in Cairo, the French sought to force him out by loosing their proconsuls against exposed British interests in unclaimed Africa, while the Germans did likewise to extort more British aid in their European affairs. Once the powers began to back their nationals' private enterprises for diplomatic purposes, commerce south of the Sahara ceased to be a matter of restricted influence over coasts; it became a business of unlimited territorial claims over vast hinterlands. In this roundabout fashion, Arabi's revolution and Gladstone's blunder exaggerated the importance of intrinsically tiny disputes in tropical Africa and brought the diplomatists to the auction rooms. . . .

In the history of Africa, the long expansion of Islam since the eighth century dwarfs the brief influence of Europe. From this western Sudan between the Senegal and Lake Tchad, between the coastal forests and the Sahara, the puritanic Almoravides had set forth to rule over Spain and the Maghreb. Here the golden empires of Mali and Ghana had risen and fallen; here Muslims and animists had struggled for centuries. Yet the difficulty of assimilating tribes into nations had foiled the making of enduring states. By the seventeenth century, Islam here was at best the cult of aristocracies lording it over a mass of pagan subjects. But from the late eighteenth century, the creed was on the march once more. United by the spread of Muslim brotherhoods with their calls for religious reform, the Tokolor and Fulani peoples rose in holy war upon their decadent Muslim rulers, riveting new empires upon the animists. At the end of the nineteenth century, when the British bumped into them in what is now northern Nigeria, their force was spent, and the Fulani emirs who had inherited the disunited provinces of the Sokoto empire were unable to resist British suzerainty. But the French had no such luck with the Tokolor and Manding empires to the west. By 1864 El Hedj Omar at the head of the *Tijani* order had brought the western Sudan from Futa to Timbuktu under his sway. When the French confronted this empire, Amadu Shehu, his successor, was imposing conformity to his version of Islam, and so overcoming the cleavage between rulers and ruled to forge a unified power. It was in the nature of such empires, founded in holy war, bound together by theocracy and the brotherhood of all believers, that their commanders could no longer command if they cooperated with a Christian power. Amadu and Samori were the prisoners of their own systems of leadership, unable to work their treaties with France without destroying their own authority. Both chose to fight rather than to abdicate. By 1889 Paris found out that Galliéni's loose protectorate meant a far-reaching military conquest.

All the traditions of the Ministry of Marine were against it. "It is the negation of all our policy," the governor protested, "...it means starting a holy war...poor Senegal." But covered by Étienne, the Algerian Under Secretary for Colonies, the local army commanders seized their chance. In 1890 Colonel Archinard broke the power of Amadu. Thenceforward protests from Paris could not stop the sand-table thinkers of the Upper Senegal Command from encompassing and crushing the embattled Muslim aristocracies one by one. In "absolute violation of orders," Archinard next invaded Samori's empire. For the next eight years that potentate and his mobile Sofa hordes kept the French army in hot pursuit from the Upper Niger to the Ivory Coast. Grappling with him and other disaffected Muslim leaders, the French were to end by occupying the entire western Sudan. Having gone so far against their will in the 1880s, logic brought them to rationalize these haphazard conquests in the 1890s. French Africa was to be all of a piece: Senegal and Algeria to be joined with the hinterlands of the Guinea, Ivory and Dahoman coasts; these in their turn to be linked with the French Congo at the shores of Lake Tchad.

For the most part, the British looked on and acquiesced. As Salisbury put in ironically, "Great Britain has adopted the policy of advance by commercial enterprise. She has not attempted to compete with the military operations of her neighbour." Her priority in Africa lay in protecting the position in Egypt and, from 1889, in closing off the

Nile valley for this purpose. In hope of damping down the Egyptian quarrel, Salisbury saw no harm in offering another round of West African compensations to France between 1889 and 1891. This vicarious generosity cost nothing either to give or to take, so Paris accepted it. The Gambian hinterland was signed away to French Senegal; that of Sierra Leone to French Guinea. But it was the Convention of August 1890 that gave the French their largest windfall; and once again the Egyptian priorities of the British shook the tree. To compensate Paris for the Heligoland-Zanzibar Treaty of 1890, in which the Germans gave him a free hand at Zanzibar and over the Nile, Salisbury cheerfully consigned to France the "light soils" of the Sahara and the western Sudan between Algeria, Senegal and the Say-Barruwa line resting on Lake Tchad. This enormous paper concession of other people's countries the Quai d'Orsay accepted with the same irony with which it was given:

Without any appreciable effort, without any large sacrifice, without the expense of exploration..., without having made a single treaty...we have induced Britain to recognize...that Algeria and Senegal shall form a continuous belt of territory.... Political access to Lake Tchad *seems* important ....It may become the nodal point for trade routes....But in striving to extend our activity towards central Africa, there is a more important consideration, bound up with more pressing and concrete interests. We want to get it recognized once and for all that no European nation can ever resist our influence in the Sahara and that we shall never be taken in the rear in Algeria.

For the colonial zealots, there may have been enchantment in such a view. But for the technicians of national security these large but unconsidered trifles were worth picking up only so far as they improved French security in North Africa, and so in the Mediterranean. Like their counterparts in London, it was not so much a new empire as the future of their old interests in Europe and the East that they were seeking in Africa. For the French this meant security in Algeria's hinterland. But it also meant security in Egypt. So Salisbury's bargains could not end the scramble for Africa. France would take all she could get in the west. But she could not afford thereby to be appeased along the Nile. . . .

In 1887 Salisbury had sent Drummond Wolff to Constantinople to make what was probably his last serious offer to evacuate the Nile Delta. The troops would sail away within three years if the powers would agree that they could sail back again in case of need. The Porte accepted. But French and Russian diplomacy combined to wreck the agreement. Salisbury pondered the meaning of this debacle. British influence at Constantinople was not what it had been. Plainly the chances of patching up and packing up in Egypt had dwindled since 1885. Despite Bismarck's maneuvers, France was now moving out of isolation and into the Franco-Russe toward the end of the 1880s. Worse still, Salisbury found that there were not enough ironclads to fight their way through the Mediterranean against such a combination. How then could the Turk be propped up against Russia? As the margin of security shrank at Constantinople, Salisbury saw the need of broadening it at Cairo. To be safe in Egypt he adopted the policy of keeping other powers out of the Nile basin. Fear lay behind this policy, the alarmist calculation that "a civilized, European power. . .in the Nile valley. . .could so reduce the water supply as to ruin [Egypt]." So from 1890 the British ran up their bids, claiming a sphere along the whole river and its approaches, from Mombasa and Wadi Halfa to Lake Victoria Nyanza. To gain as much as this, they were ready to tout compensations over most of the continent. As the British pivot began to swing from the Asiatic to the African shores of the eastern Mediterranean, the second phase of partition spread from Uganda and Ethiopia to the Zambezi river, from the Red Sea to the Upper Niger. By 1891 there was little more of Africa left to divide. The partition was all over, bar the ultimatums. . . .

It is familiar enough, the diplomacy which contrived the astonishing partitions of the 1880s; but the motives behind them are stranger than fiction. As they drew their new map of Africa by treaty, the statesmen of the great powers intended nothing so simple or so serious as the making of colonies there. There were traders and missionaries who clamored for imperial aid for their enterprises; but it was not they, it was the politicians who decided: and the politicians had no time for the notion that state action should develop the tropics in the interest of national prosperity. Trade, and the political influence that went with it, might expand in Africa; or again it might not. In either case the statesmen were happy to leave the matter to private energies. For tropical Africa at the end of the nineteenth century this meant that next to nothing would be done, for private business was as yet utterly unready to do it. Then were "claims for posterity" the objects? There is a grain of truth in this old view, but it was more a rationalization after the event. As they sliced up more and more of the continent, the politicians found it easier to explain their actions in terms of new markets and civilizing missions than in terms of the more sophisticated and less high-minded concepts on which their minds were privately running.

Those who presided over the partition saw it with a cold and detached view. It was not Africa itself which they saw; it was its bearing on their great concerns in Europe, the Mediterranean and the East. Their preoccupations were tangential to the continent to a degree possible only in the official mind. They acted upon their traditional concepts of national interests and dangers. They advanced, not the frontiers of trade or empire, but the frontiers of fear.

From a European point of view, the partition treaties are monuments to the flights of imagination of which official minds are capable, when dealing with a blank map of two-thirds of a continent. The strategists anticipated every contingency: the diplomats bargained for every farthing of advantage, while the geographers showed them the whereabouts of the places they were haggling over. From an African standpoint, the main result of their efforts was to change the international status of territory on paper. Turning *res nullius* into *res publica* made work for lawyers. It was to be a long time before it made work for Africans.

This perpetual fumbling for safety in the world at large drove the powers to claim spheres, to proclaim protectorates, to charter companies; but in almost all cases this was done with no purpose more positive than to keep out others whose presence could conceivably inconvenience a national interest, no matter how speculative or unlikely. So Bismarck had laid out a paper empire in 1884-1885 mainly to make a Franco-German entente look plausible. Caprivi had added to it in 1890 to make an Anglo-German *rapprochement* feasible. So Gladstone had moved into Egypt to protect Suez; Salisbury had laid out the groundplan of British East Africa to be safe in Egypt and Asia. In the main, British Africa was a gigantic footnote to the Indian empire; and much of the long struggle between France and the Muslims was an expensive pendant to her search for security in the Mediterranean. Perhaps the only serious empire-builders of the 1880s were Crispi and Leopold, and they merely snatched at the crumbs from the rich men's tables. For the rest, there was indeed a "scramble in Africa." But it was anything but a "scramble for Africa.". . .

Paris was to take the plunge. Like all the crucial moves in the struggle for tropical Africa, this was decided by a turn in the chronic Egyptian crisis. Salisbury had taken some of the heat out of it by simply refusing to discuss it. The French had hoped for better times when the Liberals came back in 1892, but Rosebery, the new Foreign Secretary, told Paris point-blank that the Egyptian issue was closed. In January 1893 the khedive timidly tried an anti-British coup. Cromer shouldered him back into subservience; but the crisis had its bright side for Paris. It showed that the revolutionary situation in Egypt was far from played out. It suggested that the nationalists inside the country might be usefully allied with pressure from outside to turn the British out of their citadel. The chances of external action were brightening as well. By 1893, with the Franco-Russe all but consummated, the strategic position in the eastern Mediterranean looked much more secure to the Ministry of Marine, once the tsar's warships had visited Toulon. The politics of deference were over.

Paris therefore had good reason to take a higher line in the Egyptian affair. From the diplomats' viewpoint, the partition of Africa was a large-scale example of game theory. One of the rules of the game was that control of a river's course amounted to a forcing bid for territory. So it had been on the Niger. So it had been on the Congo. Why not install a French force on the Upper Nile? The Nile was Egypt, as everyone knew. Once the *infanterie de Marine* had straddled the river, the famous Egyptian question could be reopened with a vengeance. In May 1893 Carnot, President of the Republic, revived the Brazza scheme. A task force could follow the old route towards Tchad, filter northwest through Liotard's empire of influence in Ubanghi-Shari, and then strike hard for the Nile. They would have to join it south of the Mahdists' country, since the Dervishes did not welcome visitors. But one theocracy was as good as another. Striking the river south of Khartoum would allow the French to work with Menilek, who was hunting for European rifles and sympathy. A handful of Frenchmen on the Nile would be picturesque; but joined by an Ethiopian army they would be portentous.

The contest for Egypt and the Mediterranean was speeding up again. As it did so, one remote African polity after another was enmeshed into its toils: the starveling colony of the Congo, the theocracies around Tchad, the petty Muslim oligarchies of Ubanghi-Shari, the wanderers in the marshes of the Bahr-al-Ghazal, the Coptic state of Ethiopia, the stone-age men living around the sandbank at Fashoda. As for the two European powers whose rivalry had provoked this uproar, they each strained every nerve to race the other to the dingy charms of the Upper Nile. There had been a time when light soils were booby prizes. Only the remarkable insights of late-nineteenth-century imperialism could have seen them as pearls beyond price.

But the Fashoda scheme was risky. The Quai d'Orsay could not assume that the British would sit smoking their pipes in Cairo while the French were pitching camp by the banks of the Nile; and so the policymakers in Paris held back the colonial *enragés*. To their minds, the scheme of planting the tricolour on the Nile was not a colonial scheme but a diplomatic weapon; they hoped to use it as a *bâton soudanais* to thwack the British into an Egyptian negotiation. Hence the Fashoda plan went in stops and starts, to be dragged out of the pigeonholes whenever London grew refractory. Before Paris had summoned up the nerve to carry it out, London was taking precautions against it. On their side, the British were hard at work building up positions of strength in the valley of the Nile. It was in Uganda that they were building. Goaded by the Foreign Office, Mackinnon's company had sent Lugard inland to Buganda, to tighten Britain's hold on the headwaters of the river. The country was in uproar, through the struggles of rival factions, goaded on by British Protestant, French Catholic and African Muslim missionaries. Early in 1892 Lugard managed to set the Protestants into precarious authority: but vindicating the principles of the Reformation had exhausted Mackinnon's finances, and he ordered Lugard to withdraw from Uganda. This alarmed the government. Already, military intelligence in Egypt was predicting that once the company moved out of Uganda, the French forces in Ubanghi would move in; and the Africanists in the Foreign Office conjured up French threats on all sides. To them, and to Lord Rosebery, the best defense lay in going forward. Formally occupying the country would shut out the French from the sources of the Nile; linking it by rail with Mombasa would make it a base for shutting them out of the upper valley as well. . . .

Grey publicly warned the French that any advance into the Nile valley would be taken as an "unfriendly act." Sabres were beginning to rattle. If the contention for

Egypt and the Nile had been kept on the diplomatic level hitherto, it was now to burst into active conquest and occupation. As it neared its climax, the partition, which had begun almost frivolously, became hectic. . . . Yet it was not ambitions or rivalries of this sort which drove France and Britain into carrying out their Nile strategies. It was the defeat of the Italians by the resurgent proto-nationalists of Ethiopia.

When Crispi, hoping to buttress his divided ministry with colonial success, occupied Tigré and ordered the Italian army forward into the Ethiopian highlands in 1896, he relied on the same weakness. His General, Baratieri, knew better. Italian expansion, he observed, was provoking among the Ethiopians "a kind of negative patriotism." The negus Menilek was not only equipped with modern firepower through the courtesies of white man's diplomacy; he also had the great Rases of Tigré, Gojam, Harar and Wollo behind him. At Adowa on 1 March 1896 these Ethiopian proto-nationalists crushed the Italians. It meant the freedom of Ethiopia and the fall of Crispi. . . .

Adowa so sharply transformed the politics of the Nile basin that twelve days later Salisbury ordered the Egyptian army under Kitchener to invade the eastern Sudan. . . . Even in 1897 Cromer was opposing the advance on Khartoum, as it would only lead to the acquisition of "large tracts of useless territory which it would be difficult and costly to administer properly." Plainly then they were not hastening to conquer another colony. They cautiously ordered the invasion, to forestall the French *coup* on the Upper Nile which Menilek's victory seemed to have made practicable.

This calculation was wrong but reasonable. English complacency about such a coup had rested hitherto on the hope that a French force from the west would be unable to fight its way through to the Nile; or if it did, that it would get no help from Menilek under the Italian heel; or if it did get such help, that the Egyptian army could conquer the declining Dervish state before any dangerous Franco-Abyssinian combination could take place. Adowa transformed Salisbury's view of these possibilities. Rid of the Italians, the Ethiopians were much more formidable than had been supposed; and if, as Salisbury suspected mistakenly, they were prepared to act as allies of France, they would be formidable indeed. . . .

Predictably the invasion of the eastern Sudan provoked Paris to substantiate Salisbury's fears by invading it from the west. Three months after Kitchener started for Dongola, Marchand left for Brazzaville, en route for Fashoda; and Lagarde went back to Addis Ababa to clinch the alliance with Menilek and arrange for the rendezvous with Marchand on the Nile. Whether the Egyptian army, dragging its railway from the north, could beat down the Khalifa and reach Fashoda ahead of the French seemed increasingly doubtful. So Salisbury was forced to try forestalling them from the south. He pressed on the building of the railway from Mombasa to supply the base in Uganda, and in June 1897 Macdonald was ordered to march from there along the Nile to Fashoda "before the French get there from the west." So the Anglo-French struggle for the Nile had set in motion four invasions of the Egyptian Sudan. French forces were now toiling towards it from east and west, British forces from north and south.

For long Salisbury was much more worried about the threat from Ethiopia than that from Marchand's expedition. Early in 1897 Rennell Rodd, the British envoy to Menilek, reported that he seemed very much under French influence; there seemed to be Frenchmen occupying high posts and assuming higher titles in the Ethiopian administration. In October the emperor appeared to be cooperating in sending Bonchamps's Franco-Ethiopian expedition along the river Sobat to Fashoda. In fact, Menilek merely intended to play off the French against the British who seemed a greater threat to his independence. Unknown to them, he had already made an agreement with the Mahdists. As for the joint expedition from Addis Ababa to the Nile, Bonchamps complained that "the Ethiopians did not help the mission; they did all they could to stop it from heading towards the Nile."

If Salisbury had known all this, he need not have troubled to conquer the rest of the Sudan. But, on the evidence to hand in London, things looked gloomy indeed. Having reached Berber, Kitchener found the Mahdists much stronger than expected, and remembering Hicks Pasha's catastrophe in the desert, he asked for white troops. Ministers were most reluctant to send the redcoats. But Macdonald's force, which was to have covered Fashoda from the south, had not even set out because his troops had mutinied and the Bagnada had rebelled. Like the French strategy in the east, British strategy in the south had gone astray. There was nothing for it but to press the conquest of the Sudan from the north. In January 1898, perhaps as much from fear of a mythical Dervish counterattack as from fear of the French moving on Fashoda, the British sent Kitchener his white reinforcements with orders to capture Khartoum. So at last the English army's imbroglio with the Dervishes dragged them into vast conquests of unwanted territory in the eastern Sudan, much as the French army since 1889 had been drawn into the western Sudan by their entanglements with the fighting Muslim theocracies of Amadu and Samori. In any event the fanaticisms of proto-nationalism had done far more to bring European imperialism into Africa than all the statesmen and business interests in Europe.

All these threads came together in the summer of 1898. On 2 September Kitchener's machine guns proved stronger than the Khalifa's Mahdists at Khartoum. An Anglo-Egyptian condominium was soon riveted upon the Sudan. Six weeks earlier a sorely-tried Franco-Ethiopian expedition had struggled up to the confluence of the Sobat and the Nile near Fashoda, expecting to find Marchand. He was not there. After a Russian colonel had planted the French flag on an island in the Nile, they went away. Three weeks later Marchand himself reached Fashoda. It was deserted. But not for long. On 19 September Kitchener's regiments came up the river in their gunboats and sent him packing.

At first sight it looks as though a British

steamroller had been sent to crush a peanut at Fashoda. Salisbury had spent millions on building railways from Lower Egypt and Mombasa through desert and bush to Lake Victoria and the Upper Nile; he had launched a grand army into the sands and gone to the verge of war with France—and all to browbeat eight Frenchmen. Was the Nile *sudd* worth such exertions? No less an architect of expansion than Queen Victoria herself opposed a war "for so miserable and small an object." Yet this anticlimax at Fashoda brought the climax in Europe. For two months it was touch and go whether France and Britain would fight each other— not simply for Fashoda but for what that lonely place symbolized: to the British,

safety in Egypt and in India; to the French, security in the Mediterranean. It was Paris that gave way. In the turmoil of the Dreyfus Affair, Brisson's ministry accepted the necessity of avoiding a naval war which they were in no state to undertake, even with Russian help. By the Anglo-French Declaration of March 1899 France was excluded from the entire Nile valley. In return she received the central Sudan from Darfur in the east to Lake Tchad in the west. This decided the Egyptian question in a way that the Anglo-French entente of 1904 merely ratified. With that settled, the drawing of lines on maps might have ended as it had begun with Egypt; but it was too late. By this time there was no more of tropical Africa left to divide.

III. NON-EUROPEAN ORIGINS OF IMPERIALISM

John S. Galbraith

THE TURBULENT FRONTIER

John S. Galbraith (1916-   ), an authority on British imperialism, has published several works dealing with nineteenth-century expansionism, including *The Hudson's Bay Company as an Imperial Factor* (1957) and *Reluctant Empire* (1963). He is presently a professor of history at the University of California, Los Angeles. In this selection, Galbraith examines the extent to which imperial expansion was triggered by the man on the spot rather than as a result of decision in the European capital. Faced with a "turbulent frontier," the local official in his desire to create security preferred to attack the unconquered peoples living on the frontiers of the existing colony. Often against the will of London the official proceeded and delivered additional real estate to his surprised superiors.

BRITISH imperial policy during the first three quarters of the nineteenth century was increasingly dominated by men of business and industry who prided themselves upon their clearheaded devotion to sound economic principles. The world in which they lived had no place for maudlin sentimentality. The industrial system which had made Britain the wealthiest and most powerful state in the world must not be trammeled by artificial restrictions nor should its expansion be slowed by uneconomic burdens. Their religion was Material Progress, and its high priests—Cobden, Bright, Merivale, and others—preached that the Empire was an anachronism, an expensive relic of a bygone day. Few were disposed to sever the bonds between Britain and its colonies; but these colonies must be made to pay their own way.

India was usually excepted from generalizations on the uneconomic character of colonies. The British public applauded military victories in India and consequent expansion, particularly if the campaigns were short, sharp, and brilliant, with all expenses paid by the Indians. As one journal, hostile to expansion, complained, "Public opinion in this country has not hitherto been opposed to an extension of our dominion in the East. On the contrary, it is believed to be profitable and all classes are ready to hail with approbation every fresh acquisition of territory and to reward those who bring us home title deeds." But even in India, the wealth of which had contributed to Britain's

Reprinted from John S. Galbraith, "The 'Turbulent Frontier' as a Factor in British Expansion," *Comparative Studies in Society and History,* Vol. II (1959-1960), pp. 150, 155-168. Copyright ©1959 by the Society for the Comparative Study of Society and History. Used by permission of Cambridge University Press.

phenomenal industrial growth, there seemed to be little economic justification for further expansion. None was disposed to withdraw from the treasure house of the Ganges basin, but there was no zeal in "Whitehall," "the City," or Manchester for the extension of British responsibilities in India. Yet the expansion of the British Empire continued.

This paradox cannot be explained in terms of any easy generalizations. Some have alleged that British leaders of the nineteenth century were not so steely-eyed as they professed—had they not joined in the crusade for the abolition of slavery, and were they not deeply affected by the missionary movement to Christianize the heathen? None should underestimate the romantic strain in Victorian England, but British politicians were usually disposed to give their support to policies up to and only up to the point where they involved substantial levies on the British taxpayer. The conflict between the stated policy of nonexpansion and the fact of expansion cannot be understood in terms of insincerity, for aversion to territorial acquisition was undoubtedly genuine. Part of the explanation lies in the pull exerted by "turbulent frontiers" adjacent to the area of imperial authority and in the wide powers exercised by imperial viceroys in an era of primitive communications.

In India where in the late eighteenth and early nineteenth centuries British preeminence was far from secure, wars might be fought and the issue decided before news of their outbreak reached London. The usual means of communication, via the Company's own fleet of East Indiamen, was slow even by the standards of sailing ships of the day, and still slower during war when these ships were required to sail in convoy, though in an emergency East Indiamen might make creditable time. A British journalist, hailing a sensational voyage of a fleet of these vessels from China in 1817 (109 days from Canton to the Lizard), wrote:

With similar passages we ought to communicate with our Asiatic Presidency at Calcutta within six months, instead of twelve to fifteen months, as is now the loitering and dilatory habit of that important intercourse. The Americans of New York and Washington will soon exchange letters and products with Bengal in five months! The only early account we had of the victory at Waterloo being heard of at Calcutta was from New York.

The voyage around the Cape was at best a long and arduous one. Early in the nineteenth century the passage to India by this route normally required five or six months and the homeward voyage, which usually involved a call at St. Helena, a little longer. The alternative route via the Mediterranean and the Isthmus of Suez was considerably shorter, and by 1777 Indian correspondence of greatest urgency began to be carried regularly by this route. But communication by way of Suez was uncertain and hazardous, for the overland link could be cut when Turkey was at odds with Britain, as was not infrequently the case. Between two and two and a half years usually elapsed before a Governor General of the early nineteenth century received a reply to even his most urgent communications. Consequently he was required to assume vast authority. His supreme task was the maintenance of order within his area; failure to do so was the one unpardonable sin; and in the prosecution of that objective he was often led to take actions which were not authorized by his instructions, indeed, in many cases, in direct violation thereof.

It was partly in recognition of the fact that Indian policy must largely be made in Calcutta rather than London that British authorities after the India Act of 1784 exercised such care in the selection of Governors General. Appointments to some colonial governorships or to subordinate Imperial offices might illustrate Mill's description of the Empire as "a gigantic system of outdoor relief for the upper classes," but not those to the control of British India. Lord Cornwallis and his successors had three characteristics in common—noble birth, powerful political support, and, with one or two exceptions, unusual energy and ability. These qualities contributed to the extension of British power in India. Some governors made war on Indian states with zest, others with great reluctance, but all confronted the fact that in a disorderly subcontinent the security of Bengal, Madras and Bombay could only be safeguarded by the extension of British authority, even though the areas brought under British control might not in themselves be commercially profitable. As the disintegration of the Mogul Empire in the eighteenth century had led the East India Company from commerce to conquest, so did continued turbulence on the borders of British authority make governors of the nineteenth-century conquerers on a grand scale. A mid-nineteenth-century commentator wrote:

Amongst the features by which our Indian rule is specially distinguished, one of the most conspicuous is the peculiar difficulty to which we are exposed in the maintenance of the frontier. In order to preserve the territory we hold, it has been judged necessary to keep up alliances, to interpose between rival powers, or to plunge into costly wars upon the borders. British India cannot be marked out on the map, and governed like other countries by the ordinary machinery of a domestic system. In the close neighborhood of numerous races who are at once divided against themselves by antagonistic interests, and united against us by a common faith, the government of India is as much a matter of intricate policy from without as of control and organization from within. To this curious position of an Empire won and sustained in the midst of jealous and hostile tribes, may be ascribed the fact of its rapid and still increasing extension. This extension is considered, in fact, an inevitable condition of its existence. It was necessary to advance our dominions farther and farther for the mere protection of what we already possessed. Feuds on the border must be subjugated as a safeguard against the infection of rebellion at home.

The difference in perspective on India's problems between London and Calcutta produced a fundamental conflict with regard to the necessity and desirability of expansion in India. To the directors of the East India Company and to most British statesmen, it was self-evident that commerce required peace, that war was costly, and that British governors should therefore direct their energies to preserving tranquility within their borders. To the governors, it was apparent that the commerce of British India could not be secure so long as there were rival military powers on its frontiers. By legislation and by specific instructions the Company and the government at home sought to prevent aggression, but they were repeatedly confronted with the *fait accompli* of expansion by their representatives in India.

One of the damning allegations in the indictment of Warren Hastings was that he had pursued a policy of aggression in the Rohilla war. By Pitt's India Act, the Parliament asserted that "to pursue schemes of conquest and extension of dominion in India are measures repugnant to the wish, the honor, and policy of this nation." The Governor General was forbidden to declare war or to subscribe to a treaty providing for making war against any of the Indian states without the authority of the Court of Directors or the Secret Committee thereof, unless he was defending the British territories or those of its allies against aggression. Even in such instances he was required to provide the Company and the Government with a detailed justification of his conduct.

Such a statement of policy, of course, contained two basic weaknesses. Avowedly aggressive wars by modern European states are most exceptional phenomena; every war in India was justified in terms of defense; and the ultimate verdict of the home authorities was usually as irrelevant as that of the historian. The impossibility of holding a strong governor on a short leash was illustrated by the administration of Lord Mornington (the Marquis of Wellesley). Mornington's instructions were to maintain the balance of power in India; his policy was to destroy all effective opposition to the British authority. Even before he arrived at Calcutta to assume his duties, he gave notice that he would be guided by his own appraisal of the state of India rather than by the instructions of the Board of Control which might be both unrealistic and obsolete. From Cape Town, en route to India, he wrote to Henry Dundas, President of the Board of Control:

. . .I am aware that I cannot receive your opinions for a long time. In that interval circumstances may compel me to decide some of these important questions upon my own judgment; my wish, however, is to reserve them all for yours; and with this view I propose to pursue a system of measures which, while it shall leave all the most delicate parts of the situation of affairs in India open to your decision, shall tend to check, in some degree, the progress of the French party at Hyderabad, and to furnish me with such materials as shall enable me to form a competent opinion of the effects to be expected from any decision of the point reserved for your judgment.

As events proved, few if any "delicate" problems were reserved for Dundas' decision. The primitive state of communications made it necessary that Wellesley exercise power almost without restriction throughout his administration. The nature of instability on the subcontinent, the specific character of the French menace, and the means for the assurance of British security could not be ascertained from London. The assessment had to be made on the spot. . . .

Regardless of the character of the Governor General, the expansion of the power of British India continued almost without interruption throughout the first half of the nineteenth century. Whether policy was made by a Wellesley or a Dalhousie committed to expansion, or a Minto or a Hardinge initially inclined to nonintervention, the British authority was steadily extended over the subcontinent. Whether expansion was eventually approved or condemned, the home authorities found themselves confronted with accomplished facts which they felt required to accept. Though the Company's directors recalled Lord Ellenborough in 1843 for his arrogant disregard of their instructions and in particular for the conquest of Sind by his impetuous subordinate Sir Charles Napier, the annexation was not reversed.

Frontier policy in India involved certain complications not present in other areas of the British Empire. Not only was India the most lucrative source of revenue but it was highly vulnerable. The menace of France had been a preoccupation during Wellesley's governorship; the threat of Russia became increasingly formidable in the regimes of his successors. Consequently the problems of

order involved not merely the pacification of a "turbulent frontier" but the defense of India against the threat of attack from a powerful state. Further, governors were subject to control by two masters, and though they usually sought support primarily from the ministry rather than from the Company, they did so at their peril, as Ellenborough discovered.

The frontier problems of Malayan governors in the 1870s by comparison seemed simple—they were responsible only to the Colonial Office, and the territories under their jurisdiction, of relatively minor economic significance, were not threatened with attack by a formidable foe. They were connected with London by telegraphic communication. Policy in Malaya might consequently have been expected to be less expansionist than that in India and the governors less inclined to take independent action. But this was not the case.

The first British footholds on the Malayan peninsula were established as the result of the activities of energetic servants of the East India Company. Francis Light acquired Penang as a trading post from the Sultan of Kedah in 1786, on the Sultan's understanding that the Company would protect him against his enemies. This condition Governor General Cornwallis and his council would not accept since they wished to avoid involvement in costly and unprofitable military operations on the peninsula, but the Company retained the island and in 1800 acquired a strip of land on the adjacent mainland which became Province Wellesley. Sir Stamford Raffles purchased the island of Singapore from the Sultan of Johore in 1819 in recognition of the potential importance of a trading center and as a strategic position on the route to China. In 1824, Great Britain and the Netherlands agreed to spheres of influences by which the paramountcy of British interests was recognized on the peninsula and Sumatra was re-ceded to the Dutch. By this agreement, Malacca, which had passed between British and Dutch control since 1795, again became a British possession. The final British acquisition during the life of the East India Company was in 1826, when the small island of Pangkor was ceded by the Sultan of Perak.

These British possessions were scattered along the western side of the Malay peninsula, separated from each other by many miles and by native states where the Company exercised no authority and indeed sought to avoid involvement. The trade of Malaya was considered of little significance by the directors of the East India Company, and after the loss of the Company's trading functions in 1833, Malaya became a liability. But the trading posts remained under the control of the government of India until 1867, when they were transferred to the jurisdiction of the Colonial Office, with the stipulation that their administration was to involve no expense to the Imperial government except a small sum authorized by Parliament for defense.

Even more emphatically than had been the case in India, the dominant forces of British society seemed to be hostile to expansion in Malaya. Unlike India, there were no important British economic interests involved in Malaya. The merchants of Singapore had no great influence in Parliament, and governments of the 1860s, whether Liberal or Conservative, were notoriously averse to expenditures for colonial purposes. Yet the assumption of control by the Colonial Office was followed shortly by an active policy of British expansion in the Malayan peninsula. Frank Swettenham, who was an active participant in this extension of British authority, explained the phenomenon in this way:

. . .our connection with them [the Malay states] is due to the simple fact that seventy years ago the British government was invited, pushed, and persuaded into helping the rulers of certain states to introduce order into their disorderly, penniless, and distracted households, by sending trained British civil servants to advise the rulers in the art of administration and to organize a system of government which would secure justice, freedom, safety for all, with the benefits of what is known as Civilization.

This somewhat Kiplingesque interpretation, while it offers a commentary on the Victorian Englishman's conception of his mission, provides little insight into the nature of British expansion in Malaya. Basic to an understanding of the aggressive policy of the 1870s is recognition of the fact that while the trade of Malaya might seem small from the distance of Downing Street, it was of great importance to the commercial interest of Singapore and Penang, and the British governor, "the man on the spot," saw the problems of his administration from the perspective of Singapore rather than London, regardless of the instructions he had received on leaving England.

The transfer of the Straits Settlements to the Colonial Office gave the position of the governor far greater authority than when the Settlements had been an insignificant backwater of Indian affairs. Prior to 1867, the governor of the Settlements had been a subordinate of the Governor General of India in Calcutta, who was invariably frigid to an aggressive policy in Malaya. But under Colonial Office jurisdiction, the governor in Malaya had direct communication with London. This removal of an intermediate echelon had particular significance since governors after 1867 were usually men of action who took a broad view of their area of authority. Thus, despite the conviction on Downing Street that Britain should not intervene in the affairs of the native states, the governor by his reports and by his actions created the conditions which forced the home government to a contrary policy.

Consistently with its general policy of reduction of expenditures for colonial purposes, the imperial government wished to make the Straits Settlements as far as possible self-supporting. But the revenues of the Settlements were largely derived from trade with the native states, and disorders in these areas outside British authority inevitably reduced the revenues of the colony and necessitated greater subsidies from the British taxpayer. The home government was consequently faced with the paradox that intervention in the affairs of border states, which it desired to avoid primarily for financial reasons, was necessary for the financial stability of the Straits Settlements, which it desired to promote to relieve the

British treasury. Characteristically, the home government refused even to recognize the existence of a dilemma. The first governor of the colony, Major-General Sir Harry Ord, was consequently required by his instructions to pursue two contradictory policies— to abstain from interference in the affairs of native states and to promote the financial self-sufficiency of the Straits Settlements.

In view of the restrictions imposed upon his governorship it is not surprising that Ord's administration did not satisfy either the merchants of Singapore or his superiors in London. To the petitions of the Chamber of Commerce for protection of British interests in the native states, he was compelled to reply that the imperial government could assume no responsibility and that they must trade in these areas at their own risk. But in his reports to the Colonial Office, he repeatedly emphasized that the internal affairs of the native states could not indefinitely remain outside the purview of imperial interest, and his representations undoubtedly contributed largely to a shift in British policy.

Ord had the opportunity to present his views personally to the home government in 1871 when he returned to England on leave. During his visit to London he received further impressive documentation that the affairs of the native states could not be matters of indifference.

In June 1871 British naval officers received a report of the piracy of a British trading boat by Chinese and Malayans from Selangor. A man-of-war was sent to the scene and when an effort was made to arrest persons identified as having taken part in the piracy, a struggle ensued and shots were exchanged between the Selangor forts and the warship, the forts being destroyed. In London Ord laid before the Earl of Kimberley, the Secretary of State for Colonies, a description of general disorder on the Malayan peninsula and pointed out how he had been hampered by his instructions to pursue a passive policy. He told Kimberley that Britain could only maintain its position on the peninsula by constant supervision of the native states to ensure order. But Kimberley

was not easily convinced. As Ord described the interview, while the Secretary of State acknowledged to some extent the force of the argument, he "expressed in the most decided terms his objection to extend in any way the Governor's authority to deal with native affairs. . .He assured me that the Government would not approve of any measure entailing addition of territory nor any step likely to bring us into collision with the natives, unless it were forced upon us in self-defense, or in the punishment of any attack." This remained official policy until 1873. To complaints from British subjects, largely Chinese, that their tin-mining operations were jeopardized by disorders in the native states, the Colonial Office in July 1873 reiterated that it could not authorize the use of armed force in their behalf, and in August it repeated this position to a British capitalist who was interested in investing in a large Selangor tin-mining concession.

But not even the Exchequer minds of the Gladstone administration could be indifferent to the significance of the opening of the Suez Canal. The distance between Britain and Asia was now shortened by two months from that via the Cape route, and the bulk of the world's trade to eastern Asia poured through the Straits of Malacca. From a backwater of Empire, Malaya had now become of great strategic importance. These facts forced the Colonial Office to recognize that Great Britain could not remain unconcerned with the instability of petty principalities adjacent to the route to eastern Asia, but the recognition was partial and grudging. . . .

Sir Andrew Clarke was cast in the tradition of the great imperial viceroys, a man who believed that only by the aggressive assertion of imperial authority could the security of the British empire be safeguarded and that in the interests both of Britain and of the native peoples themselves the area of British law and order should be expanded as rapidly as British resources permitted. A man of such a temperament was not likely to pursue the cautious line of policy implicit in his instructions. Within two months of his arrival in Malaya in November, 1873, Clarke had made commitments in the native state of Perak which went far beyond the intentions of the Colonial Office.

Perak, adjacent to the British possessions of Province Wellesley and Penang, was in a state of anarchy when Clarke assumed the governorship of the Straits Settlements. In addition to the usual turmoil involving rival claimants to the throne, this little state was convulsed by a war between rival factions of Chinese tin miners which had been raging since 1872, involving great loss of life (Clarke stated that the country had become almost depopulated), enormous destruction of property, and the almost complete disruption of trade. The value of imports into Penang in 1872 and 1873 decreased by almost one million straits dollars as the result of the interruption of tin imports from Perak.

These were the conditions which led Clarke to intervene in Perak. He dispatched an emissary to mediate the Chinese dispute, who prevailed on both sides to lay down their arms, and on January 14, 1874, he concluded an agreement in Pangkor with the chief of Perak, by which one of the pretenders was recognized as Sultan and the deposed ruler was pensioned off. The Dindings off the coast of Perak were annexed to the Straits Settlements. But the most important element of the agreement was the acceptance by the new sultan of a British Resident, who would in effect be the *de facto* governor of the state, since the Sultan was bound to accept his advice in all matters other than those touching Malay religion and customs. The Pangkor agreement became the precedent for similar intervention during the next three months in Selangor, between Perak and Malacca, and Sungei Ujong, adjacent to Malacca, in each of which there were disturbed conditions as a result of rivalries for the throne.

Neither in Perak nor in Sungei Ujong were European capitalist directly involved. In both states the mines were principally owned by Chinese, who in Perak also comprised the great majority of the population. In Selangor some Europeans were interested in investments in the tin mines, among them

James G. Davidson, legal adviser to the ruler, and W. H. Read, of the A. J. Johnston Company of Singapore, but even in this area Chinese interests were predominant. Of primary concern to the governor was the disruptive effect of turbulence in the native states on commerce and consequently on the finances of the Straits Settlements. In this effort to establish order, he consciously went beyond the limits of his authority, for he had inaugurated a system where in fact the governments of the three states were committed to the charge of British officials, whereas he had been authorized only to nominate advisers at the request of native chiefs. During his governorship the Conservative party led by Disraeli swept the Liberals of Gladstone out of office, but Carnarvon, the new Colonial Secretary, was no more ready than his Liberal predecessors had been to sanction a policy which seemed to commit Great Britain to extend its authority over the independent Malay States. Carnarvon informed Sir W.F. Jervois, who succeeded Clarke in 1875, that the Colonial Office continued to regard the residential system as provisional, subject to withdrawal at the discretion of the British government, and the residents must be made to recognize that they were merely advisers to the native rulers, not executive officers. This was self-delusion, for by the Pangkor Agreement Clarke had committed Great Britain to the *de facto* government of Perak, Sungei Ujong, and Selangor. Jervois wrote to Carnarvon, "You thought a policy of advice only was in operation, whereas, in fact, from the commencement of British intervention, the government of the Malayan States, to which British Residents have been accredited, has been in greater or less degree exercised by those officers themselves.". . .

But step by step the Colonial Office found itself forced to concede that the resident's authority must be more than merely advisory, and to accept the fact that Britain as the paramount power in Malaya must be responsible for order and security throughout the peninsula. Again the "man on the spot" had prevailed.

In South Africa, Britain was also presented with a frontier problem, but of a different character. Southern Africa was of little commercial importance. Before the discovery of diamonds and gold, the only significant material of British interest was in the harbors of the Cape peninsula, which in British hands offered a haven and a refitting base for ships on the way to India and the East, but which if controlled by a hostile power could threaten the lines of communication between Britain and Asia. The third Earl Grey, known to his contemporaries as an imperially-minded statesman, had this estimate of the Cape:

Few persons would probably dissent from the opinion that it would be far better for this country if the British territory in South Africa were confined to Cape Town and to Simon's Bay. But however burdensome the nation may find the possession of its African dominions, it does not follow that it can now cast them off, consistently with its honour and duty. It has incurred responsibilities by the measures of former years, which cannot be so lightly thrown aside.

If from the moment of the conquest of the Cape from the Dutch, the British government had resolutely adhered to the policy of preventing an advance of the then colonial frontier, and of limiting, instead of increasing, the extent of territory that was occupied by British subjects, I believe it would not have been impossible (though certainly it would have been very difficult) by judicious measures to have accomplished this object.

In his wistful reference to the "might-have-been" of stabilized frontiers Grey reflected the general viewpoint not only of his predecessors in Downing Street but of Dutch home administrations since the days of Van Riebeeck. But the environment of southern Africa was not congenial to such dreams. Since the seventeenth century settlers had trekked and governors had sought, without success, to confine them within fixed boundaries. Trek is the central theme of South African history—the Great Trek of the 1830s differed from other migrations primarily in terms of its political consequences. The expansion of the European pastoralists to the northeast and their collision with the southward moving Bantu produced problems the solution of which were beyond the powers of any imperial governor. Ridden by a home government constantly demanding rigid economy, and harassed by pressure, particularly after the end of the Napoleonic Wars, for the reduction of the number of imperial troops, Cape governors could not provide the resources to police the area of conflict. . .Governors sought for the stabilization of the frontier, the segregation of the Bantu and settler populations. The attainment of this objective was beyond their powers but in pursuing it they were drawn to expansion.

The colony at the Cape of Good Hope was the graveyard of governors' reputations. Men arrived with illustrious records and departed besmirched with varying degrees of failure, usually as a result of their inability to provide stability at minimum expense to the British taxpayer. The impossibility of the governor's position is illustrated by the governorship of Lord Charles Somerset (1814-1829).

Though Somerset was temperamentally unqualified to be a governor, he was not without ability and energy, and the failure of his frontier policy can be attributed in as great measure to the penury of the home government as to his personal inadequacy. At the time of his appointment the official boundary lay along the Fish River amidst hilly, wooded country across which Bantu and Boer raiders constantly engaged in cattle-raiding expeditions, despite the establishment of fortified posts by Sir John Cradock, Somerset's predecessor. Somerset sought to promote stability by a new policy. He would control the settler population, and Gaika, whom he recognized as paramount chief of the Xhosa tribes, would with the assistance of other chiefs keep the tribesmen within bounds. In his assumption that Gaika could be held responsible for the actions of the tribes beyond the Fish River, Somerset betrayed a complete lack of comprehension of Bantu social organization. The Xhosa tribes lived in loose association with each other with no central authority able to compel obedience. But he intelligently assessed the requirements of effectively polic-ing the colonial side of the frontier. Recog-nizing the inadequacy of fixed fortifications and slow-moving infantry as a means of apprehending marauders who knew the ter-rain, he stationed cavalry at strategic points. The requirements of security at the Cape, however, clashed with the dictates of eco-nomy at home. Somerset believed that the minimum imperial garrison for the security of the Cape must be at least 4000 men of which not less than 1100 would be stationed on the eastern frontier. The War Office, under pressure from a Parliament anxious to return to a peacetime footing after the Napoleonic Wars, decreed that only 2400 troops would be retained in southern Africa. When war broke out with a section of the Xhosa who had overthrown Gaika, the regu-lar forces at Somerset's disposal were inade-quate, and the enemy threatened the city of Grahamstown before they were repulsed. At the end of the war, Somerset sought to solve the frontier problem by another expedient— the withdrawal of the Bantu from the country between the Fish and Keiskamma Rivers. This territory was known tradition-ally as the "neutral belt," but the adjective is erroneous. It was apparently Somerset's intention from the first to promote coloni-zation of the territory by Europeans, which was treated as ceded territory. By 1825 farms dotted the area and within ten years of the "agreement" with Gaika, the Cape government officially extended the boun-dary of the colony to the Keiskamma. As the borders of European settlement were pressed forward, the lands of the Xhosa were further compressed by the incursions into their territories of refugees fleeing from the scourge of Chaka and his Zulus to the north, and disorders on the frontiers were conse-quently aggravated. There was the familiar spectacle of the withdrawal of a less ad-vanced society before the Europeans, and its eventual subjugation. . . .

The process of expansion for security continued. Governor Napier finally prevailed upon the British government to annex Natal in 1843, partly because of the threat to British commerce if Port Natal were in hostile hands, partly because of the aggrava-tion of the Cape's frontier problems by the policies of the Natal *volksraad,* and after the Kaffir War of 1846-47, Sir Harry Smith re-annexed to the Crown the territory which Glenelg a decade earlier had forced D'Urban to disgorge. . . . Less than two months after his arrival at the Cape and without authori-zation from the Colonial Office, Smith annexed the territory beyond the Orange River inhabited by the Trekker Boers. His justification for the action in a letter to Grey is a classic expression of the "man on the spot's" reaction to the problem of the turbulent frontier:

My position has been analogous to that of every Governor General who has proceeded to India. All have been fully impressed with the weakness of that policy which extended the Company's posses-sions, and yet few, if any, especially the men of more gifted talents, have ever resigned their govern-ment without having done that, which however greatly to be condemned by the theory of policy, circumstances demanded and imperatively imposed upon them. Such has been my case.

The security of all countries within depends not only upon their security from without and the existence of a relationship on the border calculated to inspire confidence. For this reason I brought British Kaffraria under the protection of Her Majesty, enforcing that protection by military occupation, and beyond the Orange River I have proclaimed the sovereignty of the Queen because it affected not only the well-being of the colony, but the interests and welfare of so many thousands of Her Majesty's (in their hearts loyal sub-jects). . . With respect to the natives, I can safely assert that the measure conduces to their benefit and protection, of which they are fully sensible.

Unfortunately for Smith, he initiated his forward policy in South Africa at a time when Parliamentary demands for economy were at their height and his military re-sources were inadequate to maintain order along a vast frontier. The result was a long, harassing, and expensive Kaffir War and the reversal of Smith's policy of annexation by a British government determined to disengage itself from involvement in the hinterland of southern Africa which in the words of Gladstone had ensured the recurrence of wars "with a regularity which is perfectly astounding."

The vacillations of British policy in South Africa during the first half of the nineteenth century cannot be explained simply in terms of the difference in perspective at Downing Street and at Cape Town as to the nature and solution of the frontier problem. The tortured history of South Africa is a product of the collision of a number of contending forces. But it was on the frontier that these antagonisms focused with high intensity, and in the formulation of their views on the means to the achievement of order the Colonial Office and the Cape governors were subject to very different influences.

Clearly, also, the specific frontier problems confronted by administrators at the Cape differed widely from those of Indian and Malayan governors. The missionary movement influenced frontier policy in southern Africa but was of little or no significance in Indian or Malayan expansion. In neither India nor Malaya was there a large white settler population. Strategic considerations played a more important part in India where the threat of France, succeeded by that of Russia, subjected the British rulers to perils of far greater magnitude than those of British Malaya or Cape Colony, and the importance of India to British society dwarfed that of the other dominions of the Crown. The purpose of this discussion has not been to provide a single explanation for British expansion in the first three quarters of the nineteenth century, but rather to call attention to the importance of a sometimes neglected factor which influenced policy in varying degrees in different areas of the British empire.

In India, Malaya, and South Africa governors, charged with the maintenance of order, could not ignore disorder beyond their borders, turbulence which pulled them toward expansion. This influence was not imperative; some governors resisted it while others, if they did not welcome opportunities for the extension of British authority, were strongly susceptible to seduction. Seldom did the London government initiate frontier policy; rather, it reacted to the policies of its governors. . . .In general, while the home authorities might grumble at the impetuosity of their overseas representatives they were not disposed to restore conquered territories, particularly if acquisition and administration involved no great expense to British taxpayers. In India, Malaya, and South Africa, British dominion implied expansion, though anti-expansionists sought to avoid acceptance of the corollary. Governors continued to try to eliminate the disorderly frontier by annexations which in turn produced new frontier problems and further expansion. The "turbulent frontier" consequently contributed to the paradox of the nineteenth-century empire that "grew in spite of itself."

Ronald Robinson

"NON-EUROPEAN FOUNDATIONS"

Ronald Robinson, already represented in this volume, here argues that it is a mistake to view European expansion solely in terms of European motives and goals. Given the limited power that European states used against Africans and Asians, the success of European penetration must be understood in terms of the motives and needs of the local indigenous populations. Often these peoples collaborated, encouraging European penetration for their own reasons. This applied to both ruling political and economic elites and to specific ethnic groups, who could thus ensure or win predominance over their subjects or neighbors.

THE FEARFUL symmetry of old theories of imperialism. . .confounded the politics of empire with the economics of capitalism. Since they were invented, nevertheless, perspective has lengthened and decolonization has shattered many of their impenetrably Eurocentric assumptions. A more historical theory of the working of European imperialism in the nineteenth and twentieth centuries is badly needed.

The old notions for the most part were restricted to explaining the genesis of new colonial empires in terms of circumstances in Europe. The theory of the future will have to explain, in addition, how a handful of European proconsuls managed to manipulate the polymorphic societies of Africa and Asia and how, eventually, comparatively small, nationalist elites persuaded them to leave.

There is, however, a more compelling reason to grope for a better synthesis than those of the old masters. Today their analyses, deduced more from first principle than empirical observation, appear to be ideas about European society projected outward, rather than systematic theories about the imperial process as such. They were models in which empire-making was conceived simply as a function of European, industrial political economy. Constructed on the assumption that all active components were bound to be European ones, which excluded equally vital non-European elements by definition, the old theories were founded on a grand illusion.

Any new theory must recognize that imperialism was as much a function of its victims' collaboration or non-collaboration—of their indigenous politics, as it was of European expansion. The expansive forces generated in industrial Europe had to combine with elements within the agrarian societies of the outer world to make empire at all practicable.

To explore this more realistic first assumption as a basis for a fresh approach, is the object of this essay. It makes no pretension to accomplishing such a theory. It does suggest, however, that researches in the subject might take a new direction. The

Excerpts from Ronald Robinson, "Non-European Foundations of European Imperialism: Sketch for a Theory of Collaboration," Roger Owen and Bob Sutcliffe, eds., *Studies in the Theory of Imperialism* (London, 1972), pp. 118-124, 126-132, 138-140. Reprinted with permission.

revised, theoretical model of imperialism has to be founded on studies of the nature and working of the various arrangements for mutual collaboration, through which the external European, and the internal non-European components cooperated at the point of imperial impact. Before reflecting on this idea, it is necessary to set it in a broader context.

A definition of modern imperialism

Imperialism in the industrial era is a process whereby agents of an expanding society gain inordinate influence or control over the vitals of weaker societies by "dollar" and "gunboat" diplomacy, ideological suasion, conquest and rule, or by planting colonies of its own people abroad. The object is to shape or reshape them in its own interest and more or less in its own image. It implies the exertion of power and the transfer of economic resources; but no society, however dominant, can manhandle arcane, densely-peopled civilizations or white colonies in other continents simply by projecting its own main force upon them. Domination is only practicable insofar as alien power is translated into terms of indigenous political economy.

Historically European imperialism might be defined as a political reflex action between one non-European, and two European components. From Europe stemmed the economic drive to integrate newly colonized regions and ancient agrarian empires into the industrial economy, as markets and investments. From Europe also sprang the strategic imperative to secure them against rivals in world power politics. As the stock-in-trade of the old masters, these may be taken for granted, although of course they were indispensable to the process.

Their role, however, has been exaggerated. They did not in themselves necessitate empire. If they had one, the territorial scrambles of the later nineteenth century would have taken place in the Americas, where Europe was investing the bulk of its exported economic and human resources, rather than in Africa and Asia. One country can trade with another and be interested strategically in it without intervening in its politics. There was nothing intrinsically imperialistic about foreign investment or great power rivalry. European capital and technology, for example, strengthened the independence of Japan and the Transvaal, at the same time as they undermined that of Egypt. The great power rivalry that carved up Africa also stopped the "slicing of the Chinese melon" and delayed Ottoman partition. It ought to be commonplace, therefore, that from beginning to end imperialism was a product of interaction between European and extra-European politics. European economic and strategic expansion took imperial form when these two components operated at cross-purposes with the third and non-European component—that of indigenous collaboration and resistance. The missing key to a more historical theory perhaps is to be found in this third element.

If this triple interaction in large measure made imperialism necessary and practicable, its controlling mechanism was made up of relationships between the agents of external expansion and their internal "collaborators" in non-European political economies. Without the voluntary or enforced cooperation of their governing elites, economic resources could not be transferred, strategic interests protected or xenophobic reaction and traditional resistance to change contained. Nor without indigenous collaboration, when the time came for it, could Europeans have conquered and ruled their non-European empires. From the outset that rule was continuously resisted; just as continuously native mediation was needed to avert resistance or hold it down. Indian sepoys and Indian revenue, for example, conquered and kept for the Raj the brightest jewel in the imperial crown. China and Japan, on the other hand, provided no such collaborators as India and so, significantly, could not be brought under the yoke.

It is easy to mistake the source of the power upholding these African and Asian colonial empires. Their serried panoplies [ranks of armored soldiers] might indicate that it came from Europe. But had it come thence they would have remained paper tigers. Although potentially the power was there in Europe, in reality only a tiny fraction of it was ever committed to Africa or Asia. Europe's policy normally was that if empire could not be had on the cheap, it was not worth having at all. The financial sinew, the military and administrative muscle of imperialism was drawn through the mediation of indigenous elites from the invaded countries themselves.

Its central mechanism, therefore, may be found in the systems of collaboration set up in preindustrial societies, which succeeded (or failed) in meshing the incoming processes of European expansion into indigenous social politics and in achieving some kind of evolving equilibrium between the two.

The idea of collaborating or mediating elites

As the agents of large-scale industrial civilization invaded small-scale agrarian societies, the allure of what the big society had to offer in trade, capital, technology, military or diplomatic aid, or the fear of its vengeance, elicited indigenous political and economic "collaborators." It should be stressed that the term is used in no pejorative sense. From the standpoint of the collaborators or mediators the invaders imported an alternative source of wealth and power which, if it could not be excluded, had to be exploited in order to preserve or improve the standing of indigenous elites in the traditional order. As the cases of Japan from 1858 to 1867 and of Buganda from 1886 to 1900 among many other examples show, if the ruling elite chose resistance there was usually a counter-elite to opt for collaboration, or vice versa. At the same time the "bargains" of collaboration were not and could not be too one-sided or they ceased to be effective. Collaborators or not, the social elites of Africa and Asia who made up the great majority of imperialism's involuntary partners, had to mediate with the foreigner on behalf of their traditional institutions and constituents. Too drastic concessions in sensitive areas would undermine the basis of their authority and set their forced contracts with Europe at nought. The

irony of collaborative systems lay in the fact that although the white invaders could exert leverage on ruling elites they could not do without their mediation. Even if the bargains were unequal they had to recognize mutual interests and interdependence if they were to be kept. When mediators were not given enough cards to play, their authority with their own people waned, crisis followed, and the expanding powers had to choose between scrapping their interests or intervening to promote them directly. Nor was it possible for them later as rulers to deal with subject societies as amorphous collections of individuals. Hence the terms on which collaboration took place were critical in determining not only the political and economic modes of European expansion but also its agents' chances of achieving influence, keeping control, promoting changes, and of containing xenophobic reaction.

Two interconnecting sets of linkages thus made up the collaborative mechanism: one consisting of arrangements between the agents of industrial society and the indigenous elites drawn into cooperation with them; and the other connecting these elites to the rigidities of local interests and institutions. Collaborators had to perform one set of functions in the external or "modern sector" yet "square" them with another and more crucial set in the indigenous society. The kind of arrangement possible in the one thus determined the kind of arrangement possible in the other. When collaborators succeeded in solving these complex politico-economic equations, as did the modernizing samurai of Japan, progress was almost miraculous; when they failed to do so, as Chinese mandarins and Egyptian pashas found, the result sooner or later was catastrophe.

Although the mediators remained integrated in local society, in their dual role they rarely formed a united interest group or a unified modern sector within that society. Of necessity they played the part of collaborator more or less with reference to their roles in their own society. Their mutual rivalries within that society cut across their common interests as intermediaries. Hence collaborative systems tended to consist of collections of mediating functions isolated and dispersed through native society rather than of unified social groups within them. This differentiation between mediating roles and groups is plain, in that the same group at times allied itself to, but at other times opposed, the imperialists. The turnover of allies in a crisis was often remarkable.

The efficiency of this system was clearly proportionate to the amount of European wealth and power committed to it. This determined the weight of externally-oriented functions within indigenous society. Where the externalized activities were small by comparison with the traditional ones, collaborators naturally attached more importance to their traditional than to their mediatory role. The greater the resources that came from Europe the less imperialism depended on indigenous mediation. . . .

From the 1820s to the 1870s, in what might be called the external or informal stage of industrial imperialism, Europe attempted to lever Afro-Asian regimes into collaboration from outside and to reshape their institutions through commerce. Naval and diplomatic power forced their rulers to abolish commercial monopolies, lower tariffs and open their doors to the "Imperialism of Free Trade." Later, in return for loans, or under the muzzles of high-velocity guns, they were bundled into liberalizing their traditional political, legal and fiscal institutions to make elbowroom for their "productive classes" in commercial collaboration with Europe, to take over power. But in fact these "classes" rarely succeeded in doing so. Like contemporary development planners, classical economics overestimated the power of economic inputs to revolutionize Oriental society.

The result, sooner or later, was disaster everywhere except in Japan and India, already under the white Raj. In Japan after 1869 the western samurai overthrew the Shogunate, perilously modernized its quasi-feudal institutions and exploited neotraditionalist nationalism and carefully calculated bargains with the West to protect their independence on the basis of "rich country, strong army." By 1914 these Japanese collaborators had achieved what otherwise only white colonists seemed able to achieve. They succeeded in translating the forces of western expansion into terms of indigenous politics. By adapting European-style techniques and institutions, they managed to control them so that they strengthened instead of destroying Japanese government, and worked not for imperialism, but for Japan.

In contrast, the collaborative mechanism in China worked superficially. Admittedly the timing of the mid-nineteenth-century European breakin was unfavourable, for China was then in the grip of a demographic crisis. The mandarin bureaucracy was challenged by widespread peasant revolt from the Tai-Pings and Muslims; and in suppressing them, the central government lost its power to provincial warlords and gentry. They used it to defend the traditional order against collaborators' efforts to reform Chinese institutions from above. Free-trade imperialism enabled European merchants in the treaty ports, in partnership with Chinese merchants, to take over the exposed riverine and maritime branches of Chinese domestic trade; but the Manchu regime rejected European capital and railways and so the export-import sector hardly dented the vast, introverted domestic economy. When K'ang Yu-wei in 1898 attempted to recentralize Manchu government and to substitute Western for Confucian education in imitation of the Japanese, the traditionalist bureaucracy and gentry in effect vetoed all his decrees. And when rival European powers attempted to inject capital and railways forcibly into the society between 1895 and 1900, the dramatic xenophobic reaction of the Boxers drove them back, beleaguered, into the legations of Pekin.

From the conservative reform period of the sixties and seventies to the abortive military recentralization of Yuan Shi-k'ai in the 1900s, the indigenous modernizers and collaborators within the Manchu regime remained prisoners of the impenetrably Confucian social units that connected lower bureaucracy with provincial gentry and peasantry. This had once been an imperial system of peasant control. It had turned into a system of popular defiance, cancelling Pekin's collaborative bargains with the West. Modern ideas, military techniques, capital and institutions, therefore, could by no means be translated into terms of indigenous political processes. The railways planned too late to reimpose the control of Pekin, the modern artillery, the battleships and the loans, provoked deeper provincial and populist resistance; so that the Manchu regime continued to crumble until it fell in the revolution of 1911.

In the Muslim societies of the Ottoman empire, Egypt and Tunis, however, collaborating regimes were at first more successful than in China. By the 1850s and 1860s international free trade and capital investment had made a considerable impression on their economies through the enforced collaboration of traditional rulers and the commercial partnership of Levantine urban classes. Rulers tried strenuously to modernize their armies and navies and to exploit railways in order to strengthen their grip on rebellious provinces or conquer new ones. But the Ottoman regime consisted of a Muslim military autocracy and a Turkish heartland ruling over a multiracial empire disrupted by Slav nationalists, Armenian Christians and Arab dissidents. A handful of cosmopolitan Turks, the majority of them in the army—the main source of modernizers in Muslim states—tried to secularize the constitution and give non-Muslims equal representation and equality of opportunity within the regime. The reforms decreed by Resid Pasha in 1839 and by Midhat and Huseyin Avni after the coup of 1876 at Constantinople however, like K'ang Yu-wei's in the China of 1898, were smothered at birth in xenophobic reactions from traditional elites. The tanzimat [nineteenth-century Ottoman] reformers attempted to do so much more than the Chinese. They ended up doing much worse. The Hamidian traditionalist reaction of pan-Islamism and pan-Turkism after 1876 was that much more passionate. If the Turkish collaborators were eventually ineffective, European statesmen and bankers who dealt them a bad hand to play in Ottoman politics were largely to blame.

The character of Afro-Asian collaboration

Some of the reasons why Afro-Asian collaborative mechanisms worked differently from white colonial systems are obvious from these examples. Afro-Asian economies, being largely undifferentiated from their sociopolitical institutions, were more or less invulnerable to the play of the international market. The institutional barriers to economic invasion proved intractable; economic reform was subject to the political veto of social conservatism; as a result the export-import sector normally remained a tiny accretion on traditional society, and this meant that commercial collaborators were few and unable to win power.

In white colonies the international economy worked through neo-European attitudes and institutions which enabled their export-import sectors to convert British economic power into colonial political collaboration with empire. In most Afro-Asian examples, institutional gaps kept industrial inputs too small to empower such a mechanism. Small as they were they had to be driven in by the hammer of European intervention. External political pressure had to supply the lack of economic leverage on the indigenous political economy before a measure of economic collaboration could be obtained. Consequently the main source of Afro-Asian collaborators was not in the export-import sector but among essentially noncommercial, ruling oligarchies and landholding elites. Again, the terms of the bargain under the imperialism of free trade permitted them to divert economic resources to the purpose of maintaining the status quo, in return for protecting European enterprise and a measure of political alliance.

Sooner or later consequently these collaborating Oriental regimes fell into the international bankruptcy court as did the Ottoman Sultan and Egyptian Khedive in 1876, the Bey of Tunis in 1867, and the Manchu empire in 1894. One by one they became bones of contention between European powers, subjected to increasing foreign interference to reform the management of their internal financial and political affairs. At this point Europe had forced its internal collaborators to play for high stakes with too few cards. Its demands were cutting off their régimes from the loyalty of the traditional elites which formerly upheld them—whether they were Turkish or Chinese landlords, Muslim or Confucian leaders—until eventually popular xenophobic, neotraditional uprisings confronted their impotence. The stress of free trade imperialism within and without cracked their hold on internal politics. At different times this kind of crisis wrecked collaborative systems of the informal type in most of Africa and Asia; and as they broke down European powers were compelled to change their mode of expansion from free-trade imperialism into those of occupation and colonial rule. More often than not it was this non-European component of European expansion that necessitated the extension of colonial empires in the last two decades of the nineteenth century and the first decade of the twentieth.

The imperial takeover

Certainly a breakdown of this kind was the imperative behind the British occupation of Egypt in 1882 and therefore incidentally for much of the subsequent rivalry impelling the partition of Africa. After the imposition of free trade in 1841 the Egyptian import-export sector based on cotton grew remarkably under the management of Levantine and European merchants. Since these were extraneous to indigenous society, however, their commercial success enabled them to corrupt and exploit, but not to reform or direct, the political régime. The Khedivate overborrowed foreign capital for prestige projects, military and other nonproductive purposes, and slid into bankruptcy in 1876. Europe then imposed drastic financial controls and constitutional reforms on the Khedive Ismail in return for further loans, which alienated him from the ruling elite. When he resisted the controls to regain his popularity, Britain and France had him deposed and set up Tewfik in his place. By

1881 as a result, the collaborating Khedivate had lost control of indigenous politics to a neo-traditional reaction headed by Arabi and his colonels, Muslim religious leaders and landlords riding a wave of popular anti-foreign feeling. Confronted with the collapse, Britain and France had two choices: to scrap their commercial and strategic interest in the country, or to pick up the pieces and reconstruct the collaborative mechanism by throwing their own weight into Egypt's internal politics.

Hence it was the crisis in Egyptian government provoked by heavier collaborative demands, rather than rivalry in Europe, which first set Britain and France competing for the advantage under the new arrangements; and the lack of reliable Egyptian collaborators, rather than fear of France or any increased interest in Egypt, which brought the redcoats onto the Suez Canal in 1882 and kept them there until 1956.

In the partition of China into European spheres of influence from 1895 to 1902, the breakdown of "open door" collaboration based on an Oriental regime again played a major part. The forces which overthrew it—financial crisis, intensifying foreign intervention and anti-European reaction—looked remarkably similar to those that overthrew the Khedivate: but their Chinese sequence and combination were different. The Japanese victory over China and the war indemnity thus enacted in 1894 bankrupted the Manchu regime, making it for the first time dependent on European loans. An alteration in the eastern regional balance of power rather than European rivalry first precipitated the crisis. At bottom that alteration stemmed from the assault of Japan's revolutionary modernization on China's reactionary resistance to modern reform. It was these essentially non-European factors which called for European imperialist action. The Japanese conquests threatened Russian strategic interests in north China. Manchu bankruptcy portended the collapse of the indigenous regime. Russia with France, her ally, felt the need, and took the opportunity, to take alternative measures for securing their stakes in the Celestial Empire. Having evicted the Japanese by diplomatic pressure, they extorted exclusive spheres of influence marked out with Chinese railway concessions from Pekin in return for foreign loans, and Britain and Germany necessarily joined in the partition to save their interests.

The antiforeign reaction to intensified imperialist intervention, which had precipitated the British occupation of Egypt, helped to halt the occupation of China. The Boxer Rebellion of 1900 provoked the Russians to occupy Manchuria in much the same way that Arabi's rebellion led to the British occupation of Egypt. Shortly, however, this Chinese popular resistance, together with the Anglo-Japanese Alliance of 1902 and Japan's defeat of Russia, restored the eastern power balance and halted the imperialist takeover of China. The original necessity for it having been removed, the Chinese partition was aborted. The wheel of collaboration had turned full circle—sufficiently at least to restore the international open door system, if not to save the Manchu regime from its own subjects.

To account for the imperial takeovers in Afro-Asia at the end of the last century exclusively in terms of European capitalism and strategy is to miss the point. The transition was not normally activated by these interests as such, but by the breakdown of collaborative mechanisms in extra-European politics which hitherto had provided them with adequate opportunity and protection.

Conclusion

The theory of collaboration suggests that at every stage from external imperialism to decolonization, the working of imperialism was determined by the indigenous collaborative systems connecting its European and Afro-Asian components. It was as much and often more a function of Afro-Asian politics than of European politics and economics.

At the outset it depended on the absence or presence of effective indigenous collaborators, and the character of indigenous society, whether imperialist invasions of Africa and Asia were practicable or not.

Secondly, the transition from one phase of imperialism to the next was governed by the need to reconstruct and uphold a collaborative system that was breaking down. The breakdown of indigenous collaboration in many instances necessitated the deeper imperial intervention that led to imperial takeover. Thirdly, the choice of indigenous collaborators, more than anything else, determined the organization and character of colonial rule; in other words, its administrative, constitutional, land and economic policies were largely institutionalizations of the indigenous, political alliances which upheld it. Fourthly, when the colonial rulers had run out of indigenous collaborators, they either chose to leave or were compelled to go. Their national opponents in the modern elite sooner or later succeeded in detaching the indigenous political elements from the colonial regime until they eventually formed a united front of noncollaboration against it. Hence the inversion of collaboration into noncooperation largely determined the timing of decolonization. Lastly, since anticolonial movements emerged as coalitions of noncollaboration out of the collaborative equations of colonial rule and the transfer of power, the elements and character of Afro-Asian national parties and governments in the first era of independence projected a kind of mirror image of collaboration under imperialism.

David Fieldhouse has labeled the general idea underlying this analysis the "peripheral theory." More truly it is what might be called an "excentric" approach to European imperialism. To borrow a figure from geometry, there was the Eurocentric circle of industrial strategy making varying intersections with circles centered in the implacable continuities of African and Asian history. Imperialism, especially in its time scale, was not precisely a true function of either circle. It was in many ways "excentric" to both. It should be emphasized that the Afro-Asian crises which evoked imperialism were often not essentially the products of European forces but of autonomous changes in African and Asian domestic politics.

Changing over to a mechanical analogy, imperialism was in another sense the "center of mass" or resultant of both circles. Hence the motivation and modes of imperialism were functions of collaboration, noncollaboration, mediation and resistance at varying intersections of the two circles. It is hardly surprising, therefore, that its European directors and agents, no less than its victims, looked on imperialism as an inevitable but random process receding out of control.

What is not evident yet is a firm answer to the critical question in assessing the Third World's prospects in the 1970s and 1980s. Their international frame has altered from imperialism to formal independence with foreign aid. However, the importance of the external frame in deciding their fortunes is marginal. Their chances of stability [depend upon] indigenous politics and upon collaboration between modern and neotraditional elites. It is this factor that is likely to determine whether they become truly independent or remain victims of "neocolonialism." In overthrowing colonial regimes, how far did the nationalists of Africa and Asia merely realign the traditional and neotraditional units of indigenous politics on a temporary basis? How far did they succeed, through national party organization, in unifying and transforming them permanently? Nationalists are more "representative" of the historic entities than colonial rulers ever were, and national leaders are able to play their politics more intimately and organize them better. It is precisely because nationalists are more representative of neotraditional units that they may be in greater danger of becoming their political prisoners than their predecessors were. The experience of the 1960s suggests that the nationalists often realigned these units negatively rather than transforming them positively. That [i.e., the experience] of the 1970s and 80s may prove otherwise.

CONCLUSION

THE SELECTIONS in this reader are intended to illustrate the many-sided nature of imperialism, to raise questions and to suggest some answers. One of the first points of controversy is the use of the term "new imperialism." Does the expansion that occurred in the generation after 1880 deserve special attention? Although the motives of European expansion were not new, the speed of acquisition and the amount of territory involved suggest a quantitative difference which should somehow be marked off from the earlier expansion.

The differences were due partly to the change in the means available for overseas conquest. Europeans had developed more efficient forms of transportation and weaponry. The steamship, heavy artillery, and modern army organization gave Europeans a valuable advantage. By using indigenous troops from existing outposts to acquire additional colonies Europeans could minimize their own losses. It cost less in European manpower to acquire an empire in the nineteenth century than it had earlier. Moreover, the desire for empire seems to have become stronger. While imperialist ambitions were to be found in many maritime states from the sixteenth century on, they intensified in the latter part of the nineteenth century. Statesmen became convinced that they were safeguarding the national interest by extending the frontiers of the nation's domains overseas.

The forces that led to these convictions were many. In this collection, most essays have examined the imperialism of a single nation, or the experience of one nation in a limited region or era. But most of these experiences were not unique, and were shared by other European imperialist powers. If the British had illusions about the wealth that could be gained from empire, so did the French, the Germans, and the Belgians. The Europeans' ignorance of the uncharted parts of the world gave free rein to their imaginations. In an age of growth and optimism it was quite normal for statesmen and publicists to imagine that unexplored Eldorados lay across the seas. If, in fact, empire proved to be unprofitable, as was the case with the French and all the other powers too, enough individual businesses or other national interests were satisfied to make European states hold onto their empires and even attempt to conquer further expanses of the globe.

The controversy over the political or economic motivations of imperialism may mask the fact that the two motives were by no means necessarily opposed. Statesmen often thought of the national interest as including popular economic well-being. At a time when the national economy was expanding radically, bringing most of the population into a market economy, a statesman concerned with his country's welfare had to ensure markets for the nation, for both manufacturers and their employees. Economic strength also formed the basis of political power. In the rivalry for world power the possession of a strong economy was a valuable asset. Many of the continental nations believed Britain's wealth and power to be based on its extensive empire; this conviction induced them to follow in Britain's footsteps. Frenchmen and Germans were quick to dream of gaining their own "Indias." Emulation was a powerful motive in the imperialism of the era.

If economic and political motives were intertwined, so were government and business. Statesmen interested in winning control over specific regions sometimes found businessmen to be useful tools for the penetration and preparation of areas for conquest. In such cases, as Guillen reveals, business and government worked hand in glove. But this was not always the case. Some businessmen were inveterate supporters of overseas expansion, but others were not; business did not form a solid pressure group in favor of imperialism. And those who favored it often found it difficult to translate their desires into government policy. The business groups that favored expansion were often the weaker, marginal retailing companies. They could rarely exert enough pressure to move a government. Government had many conflicting demands to resolve, which allowed them to arbitrate between competing groups and to reach decisions relatively freely. It turns out that, contrary to what Hobson thought, banks did not favor empire unconditionally. On the whole they were conservative in their investment policies and shunned areas that were still insecure and low in yield.

If the business sector as a whole played a less prominent role than has often been ascribed to it, economic considerations still were important. Statesmen launched into empire partly because they thought it would be profitable. Statesmen would assess the worth of an area overoptimistically, and even if it were not immediately profitable, they assumed it would be in the long run. Economic calculations played an important role, but they were more the product of the chancelleries than of the stock exchanges of Europe.

The factors that produced social imperialism seem to have been important not only in Germany but also in the rest of Europe. Increased labor organization and literacy seemed to portend class conflict, and statesmen saw empire as the solution. A French prime minister proclaimed, "If we wish to conserve our social institutions, there is one method—let us colonize." Cecil Rhodes declared, "I have always maintained that the British Empire is a matter of bread and butter. If you wish to avoid civil war then you must become an imperialist." Italians wanted to colonize because they suffered from overpopulation; the British likewise thought their growing population made expansion imperative. France had a stable population, but that was also seen as a reason for empire; colonization, some imperialists argued, would create a dynamic challenge that would stimulate an increase in France's population.

The social imperialist interpretation of European expansion stresses the social forces of the era. What seems more important in the long run, however, was the statesmen's perception of the social reality. It is relatively unimportant whether European society was on the brink of a class war (it was not) and whether empire would have averted this struggle. Rather, what is important in understanding social imperialism is that some statesmen feared increased class polarization and believed that colonies were the cure. The same is true of the economic motives: while it is debatable whether colonies were profitable, it is generally agreed that statesmen believed them to be economically productive. The state of mind of the main actors is what is truly significant.

There was always something unique about every statesman and every conquest of a colony. But even the strange case of Leopold II was not totally incomparable. Few scoured the globe as indiscriminately as Leopold did in search of a colony—any colony. Yet by the end of the nineteenth century, men like Joseph Chamberlain in England and Eugène Etienne in France were similarly possessed by an imperialist passion, and found it quite natural to solve all conflicts with non-Europeans by resort to force and to reduce non-European states to subject territories.

With regard to the strategic argument, Britain and France were obsessed with such considerations in Egypt, West Africa, and Southeast Asia. Germany also dreamed of establishing its own *Mittelafrika,* a central African belt of territory, stretching from the Cameroons in the West to Tanganyika in the East.

The rivalry of the European powers was sharpened by technological innovations. The installation of the telegraph meant that policymakers in European capitals could be quickly informed of their rivals' activities. Formerly Europe heard of particular explorations or expeditions only after they had already met with success or failure. After the installation of the telegraph the speed of communications increased the level of anxiety among European statesmen. As soon as a foreign expedition was launched, its progress was charted and its meaning to the national interest was weighed. The introduction of steamships and powerful artillery meant that colonial expeditions could be brief and the advance of a rival state far quicker than in an earlier period. Failure to move meant abandoning a potential colony to a rival. The very speed of conquest meant that decisions had to be made hurriedly, often by officials with minimal knowledge of the area concerned. But an area might be valuable—one never knew. Preemption became the basic policy. Lord Rosebery spoke of "pegging out claims for the future." A French enthusiast of empire explained France's headlong dash into Central Africa by recalling, "Above all, we had to get there first." These irrational political, economic, and geopolitical fears of statesmen mutually contributed to the partition of the globe. But not all events were willed by Europe or the result of a premeditated policy in London or Paris. There were forces on the periphery that led to empire building. Political or economic groups with whom Europeans had been in contact for decades suddenly vanished because of internal coups or other social and economic crises. This created a vacuum which sucked the Europeans into a maelstrom of activity often ending in conquest.

Other forces were also at play. The turbulent frontier affected the growth not only of the British empire but of most other empires as well. European officials were concerned with the security of the existing colonies. When the nearly inevitable conflicts between a colony and a neighboring people occurred, the officials decided to quell disturbances, thus expanding the size of the European possession. Often they deliberately flouted orders from the home office. By moving to stabilize the existing frontier, French officials in Cochinchina and Senegal annexed Indochina and the Western Sudan in the 1880s. White settlers were also a force for expansion. Desiring access to new internal markets and labor forces, they agitated for expansion in both Southern and Northern Africa.

The final selection insists on the need to remember the indigenous societies and the role they played in shaping the timing and extent of European conquest. European imperialism consisted of an intricate interplay among Europeans at home and overseas, but also, of course, between Europeans and non-Europeans. Since the age of imperialism created a more closely-linked global society, it is only natural to use the perspective of world history.

The unified concept of imperialism is a construct created after the fact by statesmen, apologists, or historians. "Imperialism" is a convenient term to describe European expansion, but a single explanation for so complex and varied a phenomenon is inadequate. The size of the regions annexed, the variety of factors involved, and the long period over which the development of empire occurred militate against accepting a single interpretation. Like so much of human activity, imperialism was a complex, multifaceted phenomenon.

The imperialism of the nineteenth century continues to be hotly debated. New perspectives and scholarship should lead to a more precise theoretical formulation accurately reflecting the rich variety of experiences subsumed under the term "imperialism."

SUGGESTIONS FOR ADDITIONAL READING

A VERY EXTENSIVE literature on imperialism exists; it would be quite impossible to survey all of it. Offered here are suggestions for further reading on particular related topics. Bibliographical treatment is available in John P. Halstead and Serafino Porcari, eds., *Modern European Imperialism: A Bibliography of Books and Articles*, 2 vols. (Boston, 1974), which supersedes L. J. Ragatz, *The Literature of European Imperialism, 1815-1939* (Washington, 1944). Regular updates on the historical literature of imperialism can be found in the *Historical Abstracts* and the *International Bibliography of Historical Sciences*.

Some specialized journals are devoted to the imperial history of individual countries: the *Journal of Imperial and Commonwealth History* (Britain), *French Colonial Studies* and the *Revue française d'histoire d'outre-mer (France)*, and the *Bulletin de l'Académie royale des sciences d'outre mer* (Belgium). Articles, book reviews, and bibliographies in these journals permit the researcher to stay abreast of the latest developments.

Since the main theoretical writings on imperialism have shaped our thinking about the topic, an acquaintance with them is useful. John Hobson's classic *Imperialism* (1902) has been issued in paperback by the University of Michigan Press (Ann Arbor, 1965). Lenin's *Imperialism, the Highest Stage of Capitalism* (1916) is available in an American edition (New York, International Publishers, 1969). Many Marxist thinkers have contributed to an economic interpretation of imperialism, including R. Hilferding, *Das Finanzkapital* (Vienna, 1910) and Rosa Luxemburg, *The Accumulation of Capital* (New York, 1964). The most influential theoretical alternative to the economic interpretation is Joseph A. Schumpeter, *Imperialism and Social Classes* (New York, 1951). Good surveys of the various theories of imperialism have been offered by two

Marxists, Tom Kemp, *Theories of Imperialism* (London, 1967) and Alan Hodgart, *The Economics of European Imperialism* (New York, 1977), as well as by an anti-Marxist, E. Winslow, *The Pattern of Imperialism: A Study in the Theories of Power* (New York, 1948). Of great value to an understanding of imperialism is a history of the word itself by R. Koebner and H.D. Schmidt, *Imperialism: The Story and Significance of a Political Word, 1840-1960* (Cambridge, 1964).

Several books of readings, consisting of excerpts from major theoretical and historical works, are useful introductions to the field. Among the more valuable are Harrison M. Wright, ed., *The "New Imperialism" — Analysis of Late Nineteenth-Century Expansion* (New York, 1961); Raymond F. Betts, ed., *The "Scramble" for Africa, Causes and Dimensions of Empire* (New York, 1966); and a collection of essays on European expansion since the sixteenth century in George H. Nadel, ed., *Imperialism and Colonialism* (New York, 1964). The British experience in the nineteenth century is examined in Robin W. Winks, ed., *British Imperialism* (New York, 1963). The same editor has issued an excellent collection of excerpts from the writings and speeches of the European imperialists and theorists, entitled *The Age of Imperialism* (Englewood Cliffs, N.J., 1969). Wider in focus and including documents both on conquest and European rule is Philip D. Curtin, ed., *Imperialism* (New York, 1971). The problem of economic imperialism is elucidated in a collection of essays by supporters and critics of Hobson's and Lenin's theories: Kenneth E. Boulding and Tapan Mukerjee, eds., *Economic Imperialism* (Ann Arbor, 1972).

Several one-volume historical works have surveyed European imperialism. Among the most successful are Raymond F. Betts, *The False Dawn—European Imperialism in the Nineteenth Century* (Minneapolis, 1975), which sees imperialism as multicausal, and David Fieldhouse, *The Colonial Empires from the Eighteenth Century* (New York, 1967) and *Economics and Empire, 1830-1914* (London, 1973), which argue the political bases of imperialism, especially stressing the "peripheral causes" of empire and the rivalry between the great powers. The imbalance of power between the developing West and the non-West is portrayed as the main cause of imperialism by several writers, including A.P. Thornton, *Doctrines of Imperialism* (New York, 1965). While providing a useful examination of the theoretical writings on imperialism, George Lichtheim also makes a general historical survey, essentially concluding that empire was the result of power rivalries between European states; see his *Imperialism* (New York, 1971).

One-volume general studies have been devoted to the imperial experiences of specific countries. Most notable are A.L. Burt, *The Evolution of the British Empire and Commonwealth from the American Revolution* (Boston, 1956) and Donald C. Gordon, *The Moment of Power—Britain's Imperial Epoch* (Englewood Cliffs, New Jersey, 1970); for France, Jean Garniage, *L'Expansion coloniale de la France sous la troisième république* (Paris, 1968) and Raymond F. Betts, *Tricouleur, The French Overseas Empire* (London, 1978); on Germany, Woodruff D. Smith, *German Colonialism* (Chapel Hill, 1978). On Italy there is a convenient one-volume account in French; see Jean-Louis Miège, *L'Impérialisme colonial italien de 1870 à nos jours* (Paris, 1968). The only studies in English of Italian activities deal with particular regions, such as Robert L. Hess, *Italian Colonialism in Somalia* (Chicago, 1966) and Claudio Segre, *The Fourth Shore, The Italian Colonization of Libya* (Chicago, 1974).

Works on imperial policy in specific regions have also been written; notable is the five-volume collection of essays by Peter Duignan and Lewis Gann, eds., *Colonialism in Africa*, 5 vols. (Cambridge, 1969-1975). Prosser Gifford and William Roger Louis have edited two collections of essays by leading scholars of European expansionism

in Africa: *Britain and Germany in Africa* (New Haven, 1967) and *France and Britain in Africa* (New Haven, 1971). A one-volume synthesis in the excellent "Europe and the World in the Age of Expansion" series is Henry S. Wilson, *The Imperial Experience in Sub-Saharan Africa Since 1870* (Minneapolis, 1977). Among the general treatments of European expansion into Asia are K. M. Pannikar, *Asia and Western Dominance* (London, 1953) and M. Edwards, *The West in Asia, 1850-1914* (London, 1967).

Strong individuals shaped and directed overseas expansion. A volume devoted to some of the leading European imperialists is Charles-André Julien, ed., *Les Techniciens de la colonisation XIX-XX siècles* (Paris, 1946). Several biographies of Joseph Chamberlain are available, among them Peter Fraser, *Joseph Chamberlain, Radicalism and Empire, 1868-1914* (London, 1966) and the older William Louis Strauss, *Joseph Chamberlain and the Theory of Imperialism* (Washington, 1942). In France, Prime Minister Jules Ferry played a leading role in the acquisition of Tunisia, Indochina, and Madagascar; his motives are explored in Thomas F. Power, *Jules Ferry and the Renaissance of French Imperialism* (New York, 1944) and Fresnette Pisani-Ferry, *Jules Ferry et le partage du monde* (Paris, 1962). Théophile Delcassé, Minister of Colonies and later of Foreign Affairs, also played an important role in French expansionism; his thought and achievements are masterfully dealt with in Christopher Andrew, *Théophile Delcassé and the Making of the Entente Cordiale* (New York, 1968). Leopold II of Belgium has had several biographers, including Neal Ascheron, *The King Incorporated* (London, 1963) and Auguste Roeykens, *Léopold II et l'Afrique, 1855-1880* (Brussels, 1958). Officials in the overseas areas played a crucial role in acquiring empires and they too deserve our attention. Among the British officials whose biographies have been written, one may note the following: Lord Elton, *Gordon of Khartoum: General Charles George Gordon* (New York, 1955); John E. Flint, *Sir George Goldie and the Making of Nigeria* (New York, 1960); Roland Oliver, *Sir Harry John-*

ston and the Scramble for Africa (New York, 1957); Margery Perham, Lord Lugard, 2 vols. (London, 1956-1960); J. G. Lockhart and C. M. Woodhouse, Cecil Rhodes: The Colossus of Southern Africa (New York, 1963); Basil Williams, Cecil Rhodes (London, 1938); and H. T. Lambrick, Sir Charles Napier and Sind (New York, 1952). The Frenchmen who built the empire overseas have received far less attention, but some of these remarkable men have been studied. The life of Savorgnan Brazza is examined in Henri Brunschwig, Brazza explorateur, l'Ogoué, 1875-1879 (Paris, 1966) and in Catherine Coquery-Vidrovitch, Brazza et la prise de possession du Congo (Paris, 1969); Hubert Lyautey is studied in detail in Alan Scham's scholarly Lyautey in Morocco: Protectorate Administration, 1912-1925 (Berkeley, 1970) and in the popular André Maurois, Lyautey (New York, 1931). A series of biographies of important French officials at home and overseas who built the empire are contained in Robert Delavignette and Charles-André Julien, eds., Les Constructeurs de la France d'outre mer (Paris, 1946). The adventurer most instrumental in providing Germany with its East African empire was Carl Peters. Many of his biographies were written in the Nazi period and affected by ideological considerations, but a good insight is provided in his autobiography, Wie Deutsch Ostafrika enstand: Persönlicher Bericht des Gründers (Leipzig, 1940). Not a Belgian but a Welshman by birth and an American by adoption, Henry Stanley explored and acquired the Congo for Leopold II; Max Liniger-Goumaz has provided an extensive bibliography in Henry Morton Stanley, Bibliographie (Geneva, 1972). Two popular biographies of Stanley are also available: Richard Hall, Stanley (London, 1974) and Byron Farwell, The Man Who Presumed (London, 1958).

The economic interpretation of imperialism has usually been presented by social thinkers and economists; it has also received serious historic treatment by, among others, Fabian socialist Leonard Woolf in Empire and Commerce in Africa: A Study of Economic Imperialism (London,

1920). D. C. Platt has shown that while economics did not necessarily determine imperialism, the perceptions of British statesmen that colonies would pay led them to espouse imperialism; see "Economic Factors in British Policy During the 'New Imperialism,' " Past and Present, Vol. XXIX (1968), pp. 120-138. John F. Laffey's thesis is that imperialism was carried out to fulfill the demands of business interests in search of new markets and sources of raw material. In a series of articles dealing with Lyons businessmen, Laffey has suggested their impact on French imperial policy in regard to Indochina; among these articles is "The Roots of French Imperialism: The Case of Lyons," French Historical Studies, Vol. VI (1969), pp. 78-92. The economic motive for French colonial expansion in general is described in Henri Brunschwig, La Colonisation française (Paris, 1949). Mary E. Townsend does the same for Germany in "The Economic Impact of Imperial Germany," The Tasks of Economic History, supplement, Journal of Economic History (December 1943), pp. 124-134, as does an East German historian, Fritz Ferdinand Müller, in Deutschland-Zanzibar-Ostafrika (Berlin, 1959). For British economic motives G. N. Uzoigwe's Britain and the Conquest of Africa (Ann Arbor, 1974) is an informative source. The most influential general historical work advancing the economic thesis is G.W.F. Hallgarten, Imperialismus vor 1914, second edition, 2 vols. (Munich, 1963).

Viewing the picture more broadly, some historians have seen imperialism as a social policy aimed at alleviating class tensions at home by providing outside markets. This is best argued by Hans-Ulrich Wehler in Bismarck und der Imperialismus (Cologne, 1969); for France, a similar analysis has been presented by Sanford H. Elwitt, "French Imperialism and Social Policy," Science and Society, Vol. XXXI (Spring 1967), pp. 129-148. A collection of essays by Wolfgang J. Mommsen, ed., Der Moderne Imperialismus (Stuttgart, 1971), tests this interpretation for all the main imperialist states. While finding that this interpretation works admirably well for Germany, the authors conclude that the fit .is less than perfect for other imperial powers. Sometimes specific social forces, such as demography, played a role. Demographic pressures convinced statesmen in many European countries that colonies were essential to provide an outlet for the growing population at home. This was the case with Germany; see Mack Walker, *Germany and the Emigration, 1816-1885* (Cambridge, Mass., 1964) and Woodruff D. Smith, *The German Colonial Empire* (Chapel Hill, 1978). In Italy there were also such concerns as demonstrated in Claudio Segre, *The Fourth Shore* and Jean-Louis Miège, *L'Imperialisme colonial italien*. In Britain many social theorists saw empire as a solution to ills at home; their program and motivations are examined in Bernard Semmel, *Imperialism and Social Reform, 1885-1914* (Cambridge, Mass., 1960).

Among those who specifically examine the economic interpretation of imperialism and find it wanting, are Grover Clark, *The Balance Sheets of Imperialism: Facts and Figures on Colonies* (New York, 1936); Parker T. Moon, *Imperialism and World Politics* (New York, 1926); and Peter Duignan and Lewis H. Gann, *Burden of Empire* (New York, 1967). That European capital went abroad but was not invested in the newly acquired colonies is noted as true about Britain in A. K. Cairncross, *Home and Foreign Investment, 1870-1913: Studies in Capital Accumulation* (Cambridge, Mass., 1953) and as true of all the major European states in Herbert Feis, *Europe: The World's Banker, 1870-1914* (New Haven, 1930). Revising his earlier views Henri Brunschwig in *French Colonialism 1870-1914, Myths and Realities*, translated by William Glanville Brown (London, 1966), sees French imperialism as having been a highly unprofitable venture and claims that it was never entered into for profit; rather, the search for national glory motivated French statesmen to expand overseas.

The political interpretation of European overseas expansion is probably the most prevalent among non-Marxist historians. The nationalism of European states, their desire for aggrandizement in their rivalries with one another, and the projection of their aggression overseas are seen by several historians as the main causes of imperialism. See Carlton J. H. Hayes, *A Generation of Materialism, 1871-1900* (New York, 1941); William L. Langer, "A Critique of Imperialism," *Foreign Affairs,* Vol. XIV (October 1935), pp. 102-119; Langer, *The Diplomacy of Imperialism, 1890-1902* (New York, 1932); Richard J. Hammond, "Economic Imperialism: Sidelights of a Stereotype," *Journal of Economic History,* Vol. XXII (1961), pp. 582-598; David Landes, "Some Thoughts on the Nature of Economic Imperialism," *Journal of Economic History,* Vol. XXI (December 1961), pp. 469-521; and David K. Fieldhouse, *Economics of Imperialism* (Ithaca, N.Y., 1973).

A number of historians have seen the imperialists as being strongly motivated by ideological commitments to empire. This ideology triggered expansion in some cases and always helped sustain it. Some of the best studies of imperialist ideologies are Raoul Girardet, *L'Idée coloniale en France de 1871 à 1962* (Paris, 1972); Agnes Murphy, *The Ideology of French Imperialism* (Washington, 1948); Richard Faber, *The Vision and the Need: Late Victorian Imperialist Aims* (London, 1966); Carl A. Bodelson, *Studies in Mid-Victorian Imperialism* (New York, 1924); R. Hinden, *Empire and After: A Study of British Imperial Attitudes* (London, 1949); E. Stokes, *The Political Ideas of British Imperialism* (Oxford, 1960); Woodruff D. Smith, "The Ideology of German Colonialism, 1840-1906," *Journal of Modern History,* Vol. XLVI (1974), pp. 641-662; and A. Roeykens, *L'Initiative de Léopold II et l'opinion publique belge* (Brussels, 1963).

Special groups provided support for imperialism and have also been the subject of study. For England one may note T. R. Reese, *The History of the Royal Commonwealth Society, 1868-1968* (Oxford, 1968) and I. N. Cumpston, "The Discussion of Imperial Problems in the British Parliament, 1860-1885," *Transactions of the Royal Historical Society,* Vol. XIII (1961), pp. 29-47; for France, C.M. Andrew and A.S. Kanya-

Forstner, "The French 'Colonial Party,' Its Composition, Aims and Influence, 1885-1914," *Historical Journal*, Vol. XIV (1971), pp. 99-128; Andrew and Kanya-Forstner, "The Groupe Coloniale in the French Chamber of Deputies, 1892-1932," *Historical Journal*, Vol. XVII (1974), pp. 837-866, and C.M. Andrew, "The French Colonialist Movement During the Third Republic, The Unofficial Mind of Imperialism," *Transactions of the Royal Historical Society*, 5th series, Vol. XXVI (1976), pp. 143-166. The only study in English of the German colonial society is Richard Victor Pierard, "The German Colonial Society, 1882-1914" (unpublished doctoral dissertation, State University of Iowa, 1964); in German, there is Helmut Müller and Hans-Joachim Fieber, "Deutsche Kolonialgesellschaft DKG 1882 [1887]-1933," in Dieter Fricke, ed., *Die bürgerlichen Parteien in Deutschland*, 2 vols. (Leipzig, 1968), Vol. I, pp. 390-407.

The belief in empire created strong political pressures for expansion that had to be relieved. For Germany this is argued in the case of Bismarck's imperialism. Both William O. Aydelotte, *Bismarck and British Colonial Policy: The Problem of South West Africa, 1883-1885* (Philadelphia, 1937), and, more recently, Hartmut J. Pogge von Strandmann, "Domestic Origins of Germany's Colonial Expansion under Bismarck," *Past and Present*, Vol. XLII (1969), pp. 140-159, have argued that Bismarck launched into imperialism to appeal to the Liberals' nationalism. In other countries domestic politics seem to have determined imperialism as well. In France the deep divisions caused by the Dreyfus Affair in 1898-1899 made the government fear that it was considered weak; to show its determination it overreacted and pushed for confrontation with Britain, according to Roger Glenn Brown, *Fashoda Reconsidered, The Impact of Domestic Politics on Foreign Policy in Africa, 1893-1898* (Baltimore, 1970).

The most important political interpretation of imperialism views colonies as pawns in the international power struggle. That is essentially the conclusion of Field-

house in *Economics of Empire* and of other numerous detailed studies of specific cases of imperial expansion. In regard to Germany, A.J.P. Taylor argues that Bismarck acquired colonies mainly as a ploy to win British cooperation in European affairs; see *Germany's First Bid for Colonies, 1884-1885* (London, 1938). Strategic interests are seen as motivating the partition of Africa in Ronald Robinson and John Gallagher, *Africa and the Victorians* (London, 1961); the British concern over the security of Suez led to the occupation of Egypt and then to the expansion into East Africa, and the French expanded toward the Nile in an effort to eject the British. While they explain an important aspect of the partition of Africa, Robinson and Gallagher overstate their case, and a number of severe criticisms have been leveled against them. The Robinson-Gallagher thesis has been the subject of a collection of essays; see William R. Louis, ed., *Imperialism: The Robinson-Gallagher Controversy* (New York, 1976). The rivalry between European states is seen as the main cause for European imperialism in West Africa in several volumes by John D. Hargreaves, *Prelude to the Partition of West Africa* (London, 1963) and *West Africa Partitioned*, Vol. 1 (London, 1974). Centering on a smaller region, Boniface I. Obichere, *West African States and European Expansion, The Dahomey-Niger Hinterland, 1885-1898* (New Haven, 1971), reaches the same conclusion.

Some historians have argued that political decisions were made at a much lower level. Overseas officials far from home and eager for action and promotion responded to the "turbulent frontier" and, with little regard for their superiors, conquered additional territory. For Britain there is a rich literature; see John S. Galbraith, "The 'Turbulent' Frontier as a Factor in British Expansion," *Comparative Studies in Society and History*, Vol. II (1959-1960), pp. 150-168; Galbraith, *Reluctant Empire: British Policy on the South African Frontier, 1834-1854* (Berkeley, 1964); C.D. Cowan, *Nineteenth-Century Malaya: The Origins of British Political Control* (London, 1961);

Richard A. Huttenback, *British Relations with Sind, 1799-1843, An Anatomy of Imperialism* (Berkeley, 1963); and David McIntyre, *The Imperial Frontier in the Tropics, 1865-1875* (New York, 1967). On France see A.S. Kanya-Forstner, *The Conquest of the Western Sudan: A Study in French Military Imperialism* (Cambridge, 1969) and Kim Munholland, "Admiral Jaureguiberry and the French Scramble for Tonkin, 1879-1883," *French Historical Studies*, Vol. XI (Spring 1979), pp. 81-107.

A developing field of research, which should add much to our understanding of colonialism, is the new emphasis on the non-European sources of imperialism. This school of thought argues that the non-European societies provided fundamental forces leading to European intervention. Non-Europeans were active participants rather than passive objects of European expansion. The earliest piece to suggest this line of interpretation was John D. Hargreaves, "Toward a History of the Partition of Africa," *Journal of African History*, Vol. I (1960), pp. 96-109. On a more general level this idea has been developed by Ronald Robinson for the entire non-European world in "Non-European Foundations of European Imperialism: Sketch for a Theory of Collaboration," in Robert Owen and Bob Sutcliffe, eds., *Studies in the Theory of Imperialism* (London, 1972), pp. 118-140; and for West Africa in "European Imperialism and Indigenous Reactions in British West Africa, 1880-1914," in H.L. Wesseling, ed., *Expansion and Reaction* (Leiden, 1978), pp. 141-163. A similar theme is explored by Henri Brunschwig, "French Expansion and Local Reactions in Black Africa in the Time of Imperialism (1880-1914)," in the same volume, pages 116-140.

A subject of great importance and controversy, the history of imperialism should continue to occupy the interest of scholars and students for many years to come.